FIFTY YEARS
A CRICKETER

FIFTY YEARS A CRICKETER

Richard Gordon

Illustrated by
Geoffrey Dickinson

LONDON

To
The 888,325,378 citizens in the world who must
be at least slightly interested in cricket.

First published in Great Britain 1986
by HARRAP Ltd
19/23 Ludgate Hill, London EC4M 7PD

ISBN 0 245-54375-9

Designed by Robert Wheeler
Printed in Great Britain by
Martin's Printing Works,
Berwick upon Tweed

How strongly are all these scenes, of fifty years by-gone, painted in my memory! — and the smell of that ale comes upon me as freshly as the new May flowers.

John Nyren, *Cricketers of My Time*, 1833.

Contents

Hours of Play

A MAN'S MOST DANGEROUS enemies are his dreams.
They buy him airline tickets to romantic places now swarming with tourists, marry him to girls who sleep with his friends and burn his toast, drive his brand-new Porsche at 5 mph between traffic lights, and retire him to a delightful country cottage which discloses that St Helena begins in the Cotswolds.

From our burdened orchard of pleasures we must pick what we like, not what we think we like, nor what the colour supplements tell us we like.

I love sitting in my mac on an open bench at the back of a county ground on a grey day for a mid-week match between dull sides before a pessimistically predictable gate.

It provides the peace of God which passeth all understanding of the pitiful who find cricket boring.

Cricket! Soothing unguent for a bruising world.

Cricket! It is entwined in the English double helix.

The stately march of a match through four innings, its violent twists of fortune, Test strategy evoking the long-sightedness of the Hundred Years War, and the perpetual interference of the weather, reflect the coherent centuries of our history. The recording of each game down to the atoms of each ball rediscovers the solemn permanence of the Domesday Book.

We were playing cricket in 1230. Some Englishman doodled all over a bull dispatched to us by Pope Gregory IX (one of the difficult ones). It shows a pair at the wicket with oversized bats on a bumpy pitch, flowers at each end and a tree in between. You can see the game in the British Museum.

The first Prince of Wales played cricket, at Westminster on 10 March 1300 (a Thursday). Henry VIII's schoolboys played at Guildford, where I last watched Peter May bat. Oliver Cromwell was a cricketer, genteelly christening the 'box' with his office. Pepys's Navy carried the game overseas, a scratch match at Aleppo. 'The Indians had nothing in their hands but a club like our cricket bats,' a pair of English explorers befittingly observed in the South Seas in 1743. In 1805 Eton first met and thrashed Harrow, who were playing under Byron.

'CRICKET,' Dr Johnson defined in 1755. 'From *crycc*, Saxon, a stick. A sport, in which the contenders drive a ball with sticks in opposition to each other.'

The Great Cham displays the pure ignorance he needed to confess to the lady about horses' knees.

Crycc appears in the Old English Twenty-third Psalm, of which the beautiful fourth verse should read:

> Yea, though I walk through the valley
> of the shadow of death, I will fear no
> evil: for thou art with me; thy rod
> and thy cricket bat they comfort me.

Or perhaps *crycc* was not sporting but orthopaedic? Pronounced *crytch* it meant a crutch. Philologists argue about it endlessly.

Or perhaps cricket is a girls' game?

They were mad about stool-ball in the fifteenth century. One maid aimed at the stool, another flipped the ball away with her hand, success for either scored a single. There was dreadful trouble at Maldon in Essex during the summer of 1564, through the constables permitting Sunday play. About then,

Philip Sidney's randy shepherd Will was delightfully depicting to Dick at Wilton Pastoral Show, 'She with skirts tukt very high, with gyrles at stoolball playes.' At Easter, stool-ball was played between young men and women for an omelette flavoured with bitter tansy-juice, a prize illuminated by Nicholas Culpeper's 1653 *Herbal*, 'This herb is undoubtedly under the Government of Venus.'

Stool-ball is cricket because a 'cricket' is a low stool. Mrs Gaskell's Mary Barton in 1848 kept hers under the dresser, and in the late seventeenth century a woman threw a cricket at the head of Bishop Burnet (one of the difficult ones).

Or perhaps not.

A cricket became a stool 200 years too late to be the name of the game. Philologists argue endlessly about this, too.

The ball was trundled along the ground, the batsman scoring by popping his bat in the block-hole between the two-stick wicket opposite. The breeched, broad-hatted fielders meanwhile grovelled to pop the ball in first and run him out. This caused more fractured fingers than modern West Indian bowling. An umpire's staff to be touched instead was an invention as humane as boxing-gloves. The popping-crease degenerated into a splash of whitewash.

The century brought changes in technique apace:

About one hundred and fifty years ago, a young lady was trying to bowl for her brother. She wore a crinoline dress with a long, full skirt. The skirt had hoops to make it stand out stiffly.

When she tried to bowl underarm, her crinoline stopped her arm swinging forward. She then began to swing her arm backwards and upwards, to throw the ball from above her head. Now all cricketers bowl overarm instead of underarm . . .

says my Ladybird Easy-Reading Book *The Story of Cricket*.

Cricket! The Men of Hambledon, the game's Apostles.

11

In June 1777 the village team of Hambledon beat the Rest of England on The Vine at Sevenoaks by an innings and 168. Over 25 years they played England 51 times and won 29. From their home ground of Broad-Halfpenny Down in Hampshire they grabbed players over the vast distance of a hundred miles. Horse hire was allowed as match expenses, and they went together to away fixtures in the team caravan. They dressed up in black breeches, white waistcoats and silk stockings.

They had a great publicity machine — 'Michelangelo should have painted him,' the Revd John Mitford wrote in *The Gentleman's Magazine* of square-jawed star 'Silver Billy' Beldham, who they had imported from Farnham in Surrey. Their crowds, 'consisting most likely of some thousands, remain patiently and anxiously watching every turn of fate in the game, as if the event had been the meeting of two armies to decide their liberty.' The Men of Hambledon were the first cricketers with the Kerry Packer idea.

Cricket! Lord's, England's green and pleasant bower.

Thomas Lord, the shrewd, heavy-browed, firm-mouthed Yorkshireman, laid his ground in rustic Dorset Square off the Mary-le-Bone Road, first ball bowled 31 May 1787. Beyond lay gently rolling countryside with grazing sheep; it was convenient for the Yorkshire Stingo and already had a Nursery End.

To avoid a rent-rise he moved in 1809 to St John's Wood. To avoid the new Regent's Canal — part of London's still flowing waterways which can take you from Paddington Station to Wapping — he moved in 1814 further north to the Lord's we love. He brought his turf with him like the drawing-room carpet. In 1825 he decided to sell to the property developers.

Lord's is today not stuccoed villas with Italian eaves and bosky gardens because Thomas Lord was bought out for

£5,000 by William Ward MP, a director of the Bank of England whose 278 against Norfolk stayed a ground record for 105 years. Instead arose what Nikolas Pevsner blasted as 'a jumble without aesthetic aspirations, quite unthinkable in a country like Sweden or Holland.' What a flattering fanfare to English ears!

As St Paul's its whispering gallery, Lord's has its curiosities.

The old Tavern was an ordinary pub you could wander into in winter, gazing with your pint through the back windows and affected by the snow-covered pitch as Shelley by the west wind.

Opposite runs the Tunnel, paced by Dennis Compton in demob suit in the spring of 1946 as he mobilized his cricketing ambitions, which gives a gun-slit view of play beneath the Father Time Stand. The pavilion provides a comfortable writing-room with *The Times* and the *Telegraph* and headed writing-paper, on which I always address my tax inspector.

At the Nursery End the Lord's Shop, like Alice's old Sheep's shop, seems 'to be full of all manner of curious things'. A grotto of the demolished stand opposite was 'Ma Mound's' tiny sweet shop, on big match days crammed like the tuck-shop on pocket-money day by middle-aged gentlemen sporting the vivid egg-and-tomato colours of MCC.

'Gentlemen are so odd about their clubs,' said one of Evelyn Waugh's fey heroines.

And their club ties.

The brazen tie, and its navy-blue crested variant created in 1960 for the City and the funerals of fellow-members, are sold as warily as stolen silver. You must produce your membership pass to buy even one of the ghastly MCC umbrellas. It is as useful round the neck as a false clerical collar for committing fraud, as all Englishmen enthusiastically cash cheques for wearers of the same club colours.

This is a chivalrous tradition from King Arthur, whose knights jumped the Round Table in the sixth century to whip the wimples off the fair ladies they fancied and knot them under their own chins as cravats.

Scotland created social confusion with tartans. Wales with religious sects. England with ties. Now nearly every Englishman is entitled to wear one, even if proclaiming only his employer's logo. The tie is the tap-root of the typical Englishman, depicted before the Second World War by the Civil Service:

> A nation with common sense but lacking imagination; quick to react when they feel they are being talked down to; a delight in knowing the worst yet always suspecting the worst is being kept from them; a nation of grumblers the volume of whose grumbling is in inverse proportion to the gravity of the situation; and a people who are prepared to put up with grave hardships but not minor inconveniences.

And by Nathaniel Gubbins:

> Whatever you say won't make the slightest difference to him. He will go on patronizing the poor, snubbing his social inferiors, talking of nothing but golf while the world talks of war, marrying gawky girls with faces like camels, being kind to dogs, chasing stags over cliffs, making meaningless little speeches at dinner, and enjoying vegetables any French peasant would throw to the dogs.

When the Task Force sailed for the Falklands in April 1982 the orders at Jermyn Street's top tie shop doubled. Not only regimental ties, equally old school ties, club ties, company ties, shared-joke ties. An Englishman roused nails his colours to his neck. If foreign intelligence needs to test the temper of the country, it can telephone Jermyn Street and ask how's business?

As St Peter's in Rome, Lord's has its relics.

'It says something about the game,' thoughtfully decides *An American's Guide to Britain*, 'that the museum is open during match play. Can you imagine a baseball museum that makes a point of being open while a game is in progress?'

As Lincoln Cathedral its Imp, Lord's has its joke.

The spacious pavilion semi-basement, walled with massive porcelain and furnished with splendid mahogany seating, is served by paired doors one marked OUT and the other NOT OUT.

Cricket! The only game greater than the players.

MCC was founded at Lord's in 1787, and immediately started laying down the Laws. It was the bossy Victorians who organized the game, as they organized religion, education, poverty, riches and the world.

County grounds were rolled out before the verandad shade of new pavilions. The County Championship was codified in the summer of 1873, nine counties distinguished 'First Class' and nobody allowed to play for more than one at once. The first Test was at Melbourne on 15 March 1877. Australia won.

The musculary missionary Victorians showed cricket its soul.

It is played unselfishly for the pure enjoyment of the teams and the onlookers. Opponents' centuries and catches are clapped, their ducks and cracked ribs consoled, because its achievements and misfortunes are shared by both sides, as those of life. If the result is of negligible importance, what need to question umpires' decisions, however outrageous, or risk the infamy, even bother with the trouble, of cheating?

This spirit consecrates the game whether played at Lord's, on the village green, or on ice (the crews of HMS *Fury* and *Hecla* did at Igloolik during the winter of 1822–23).

Cricket is defined equally by the dictionary of Oxford University, a struggling side, as 'an open-air game played with ball, bats, and wickets,' and 'fair play, honourable dealings with opponents and rivals'.

England saw Labour Government only because Stanley

Baldwin (sometimes smoking his pipe at the Oval) in 1929 passed the Premiership to Ramsay MacDonald's minority as 'it wouldn't be cricket' otherwise. Every Englishman knows that he must *Play up! Play up! and play the game!* whether there's a breathless hush in the Close or the Gatling jammed and the colonel dead. 'I think he would have condoned her adultery', was overheard during a 1970s Test, 'if she hadn't done it while he was playing cricket.'

This traditional identification of the national virtues with the national sport dates only from the Victorian public school explosion, institutions once defined to me by fellow-cricketer Michael Denison as 'predominantly for educating the sons of tradesmen, where Swan won't speak to Edgar and Debenham is far too fond of Freebody'.

Before the First World War cricket was as cherished for mingling beauty, good humour, whimsicality, chauvinism, manliness, simplicity and decency as was Rupert Brooke's hit poem *Grantchester* — criticized later as 'nothing but an enormous gush of "country" sentiment, a sort of accumulated vomit from a stomach stuffed with place-names,' by George Orwell, who did not shine at cricket at Eton.

The amateurs were members of the club who happened to play. The professionals were its hired servants. The gentlemen donned well-pressed flannels in airy changing-rooms, the players pulled on sweaty shirts beside the pavilion boiler. They took the field through separate gates. Why not? No gentleman shared his front door with his cook.

The upstairs-downstairs arrangement between the wars put D. R. Jardine watching play alone at the Oval in the captain's room two storeys above the uninitialled pros. If his exploitation of bodyline bowling hardly expressed the cheerful courtesy expected from opponents, the English nobs have always been more ruthless than the workers in disposing of sporting or political antagonists, wildlife, social bores or their own children.

Since the 1962 season cricket has fielded no amateurs nor professionals, only players. The game described by W. G. Grace as 'The sport of the people, open to all, from the prince to the peasant,' was the first to erase class distinctions. County, club, village and school display on Saturday afternoons our priceless heritage, the democracy of white flannels.

Modern players are not flanelled fools but men with wives, children, mortgages and a living to earn, a working life pleasant but sometimes brutish and always short. Only the few successful can larkily cut showbiz figures.

The stiff upper lip now risks implantation on the cheek of the catcher. The beautiful pictures in the Long Room at Lord's are found fakes. The bowlers triumphantly break bones instead of stumps. The crowds no longer behave like a congregation. Gallup discovered that a million English people keep for nocturnal protection a cricket bat under the bed.

The Oliver Cromwell, recently as unmentionable as a Victorian gentleman's unmentionables, frequently appears on television. One famous fast bowler is said to be the only player to have his dented from the inside. A lady cricketer declared her side's equivalent was a manhole cover.

But cricket remains what the Bishop of Hereford christened it at a dinner to its god, W.G. — 'That English game least spoiled by any form of vice.'

Cricket! It ripely fills 'late June, July and early August — fruit-eating months when the English become callous, pleasure-ridden, amorous and Elizabethan,' as Cyril Connolly seemed to think.

Cricket is England's Chekhov. Everything is desperately important, but outside the Cherry Orchard entirely insignificant. It lets us luxuriate in being earnestly casual and casually earnest. We can imagine we are still being acted by Basil Radford and Naunton Wayne and drawn by Pont.

18

When the North Sea runs dry like a pub at the end of a glorious Bank Holiday we shall stay sitting on the comfortable upholstery of our national self-delusions eating our sandwiches and enjoying the game.

For half a century my hours of play have been divided between fishing and watching cricket. I hope I am right that the gods do not deduct from man's allotted span the hours spent doing either.

I Play for Kent

I WAS SELECTED TO play for Kent on Saturday 27 September 1975.

Colin Cowdrey of Kent and England telephoned the exciting news the week before the game.

'Kipper' and I were neighbours in Bromley, Kent.

My family had been immeasurably honoured by sharing the driving of our combined children to school. The first day of term, I had sat with quivering respect on the back seat of Colin's Jaguar while C. S. Cowdrey of Kent and England (later) shared the front one with my son.

I was horror-struck. My child piped to the driver, 'Mr Cowdrey, are you a cricketer?'

Colin assured him, 'Yes.'

I wished to disappear through the back axle when my beastly boy demanded, 'Have you ever made a hundred runs?'

The sportsman the world knew, with the smile of leaving a long-hop from a novice bowler, said, 'Twice.'

On April Fool's Day 1965 something terrible happened to Bromley.

Kent disappeared.

It vanished as completely as Pompeii, and quicker.

It sped ten miles down the Hastings road, and started at Pratt's Bottom.

We lived in London.

Some granite-souled Civil Servant had displaced us at a callous stroke from the Garden of England to Herbert Morrison's backyard. The proud population of Bromley were as pathetically powerless as the middle-Europeans forever partitioned by Europe's ruthless rulers.

We could have risen like the Czechs. But one does not demonstrate in Bromley. Though I believe some sharp letters were dispatched to the *Daily Telegraph*.

Like Paderewski, the pianist who became the Polish Premier, like Jean-Paul Sartre when the Germans overran Paris, I stood my ground. The Captain of Kent could not. Kent did not suffer the Yorkshire puritanism of demanding their players to be born within the sound of Bill Bowes, but could not expect a Captain-in-Exile. Kipper sold his desirable detached residence in charming garden with many interesting features, including a fast-bowling machine, Ferrous Fred.

This was not a miracle of modern technology like the plastic Oliver Cromwell. It had appeared at Victoria Gardens, Gravesend, on the Monday morning of 9 October 1837, conceived by the Headmaster of Alfred House School, Blackheath — Nicholas Wanostrocht of the Belgian scholastic family and Kent and England, team-mate of Fuller Pilch and Alfred Mynn, Felix of *Felix on the Bat*, of the evergreen coaching manual.

The prototype *catapulta*, knocked up by a Kent blacksmith, was a powerful spring-loaded arm ending in an India-rubber tipped hammer-head. Released like a mousetrap, it hurled a ball programmed by grooves on a metal plate at a pace 'to split your bat in two'. Felix got the idea from the Romans, who, not enjoying the civilizing effects of cricket, had to use it for sieges.

The Bromley garden model was more sophisticated, and permitted me to claim regular batting against Colin Cowdrey's bowling, when it was only his finger on the trigger.

My first-class playing career started late. I was automatically

21

attracted first to soccer, perceived by C. B. Fry of Hampshire and England as 'a game appealing only to people with blank minds'.

I watched Alex James dribble, but I never saw Bradman bat. I saw Miller bowl. I was then a houseman at Bart's — unqualified, doctors in the middle of the war being as scarce as taxis.

Lord's was playing fixtures in which the enemy could participate. On the first day of Army v RAF in July 1944, the Germans dispatched a flying bomb from the Pavilion End. It overshot the wicket and went for byes at the Nursery End, being dropped in the Prince Albert Road. The batsmen and fielding side were meanwhile studying the root-system of the Lord's grass. First ball after the resumption of play was hooked by J. D. Robertson of Middlesex and England for six. This expression of the Dunkirk Spirit brought a standing ovation.

During the blitz in the winter of 1940 three bombs fell on Lord's, the ground staff expectedly filling the craters without trace. Father Time suffered war damage, but that was by the straying cable of a British barrage balloon. The Oval meanwhile was strewn with Nissen huts and entangled in barbed wire for transit prisoners of war, the Colditz of Kennington.

I wangled the day off to see Keith Miller. I settled excitedly outside the Tavern with my beetroot sandwiches (snoek was a post-war delicacy) and pint of wartime beer, which had a more sensational effect on the kidneys than the mood.

Miller took the new ball. He paced towards the Nursery End. He started his run. He gave a yell. He clutched his leg. He was supported from the field by his team-mates. I never saw him again until we met in the Cricketers' Bar of the Windsor Hotel in Melbourne during M. J. K. Smith's side's tour in 1966, but he seemed to have forgotten about it.

Ten years before my selection for Kent — on 16 June 1965 — I had been picked to play under the captaincy of Richie Benaud of New South Wales and Australia. He was skippering the Authors' XI, having recently created *Way of Cricket*, against the Publishers' XI on Westminster School Ground, an annual fixture deserving of the record books for enjoying the longest luncheon interval.

Even the most menacing English institutions — the House of Commons, the TUC, *The Times*, the Stock Exchange, the Bar, Equity — throw an annual cricket match. This is priceless public relations. No union leader, judge, chairman of the board, or Shakespearian actor ever looked in the slightest frightening photographed at the crease. The newspapers one autumn had a beguiling picture of the SDP Torquay Conference and Cricket Festival, Dr Owen at the wicket and Shirley Williams in cricketing cap crouched close behind it, both playing bravely without pads, the next two senior members of the Party positioned at silly long-stop.

Some abrasive national figures exude the public emollient of fondness for cricket as an alternative to caring for the disabled. It is a revealing virtue, for cricket-loving, unlike compassion, cannot be simulated. Falsity is soon stumped by ignorance. A man had far better admit it, if he finds the game too boring to merit the trouble of trying to tell a Chinaman from an Indian Tourist.

I declined Richie Benaud's invitation to turn out. I feel authors let the side down, packing it with cricketers who happen to have written a book. It is as pathetic a confession of inadequacy as a housewife calling in professional caterers for a dinner-party.

I had by then played cricket all over the world.

P. G. Wodehouse was writing in 1935:

This practice of ships' doctors of always grabbing the prettiest girl on board and carrying her off to play quoits or deck-tennis is one of the most disturbing phenomena of ocean travel, and it is one that has caused many a young man to chew the lower lip and scowl with drawn brows.

As a young ship's doctor I grabbed eleven of them and organized mixed cricket. This was played along matting on the boat-deck, with netting to stop the flashing cover-drive becoming a drop in the ocean.

I represented my ship against a British Expatriate XI 1,000 miles up the Amazon at Manáus, which had gas street-lamps and trams like the Liverpool we left behind us, and a lovely opera-house from which the song-birds had flown. The pitch was the largest patch of grass amid the Selvas for thousands more miles in all directions. Added to the anxiety of dropping a sitter in the outfield was encountering a boa constrictor. When rain stopped play we went aboard, everyone knowing it would continue for six months.

I have played on the tarmac of Milan Airport with James Robertson Justice. British Airways produced a bat *en route* to the Venice Film Festival when Diana Dors inflamed Europe by lounging in a gondola in a mink bikini. Such unconventional behaviour as hers today would pass unnoticed. As ours would have the airport instantly surrounded by helicopters and commandos.

I was appearing for the Punch XI against delightful village sides, where they always sent me in last man and made me field behind a tree. Serious reflection about batting No. 11 for a comic magazine decreed my retirement from the game. I played my last innings in mid-Sussex between tea and opening time. I made 3, all off the top edge, between the wicket and the wicket-keeper, scoring strokes I dare to claim beyond Denis Compton in his brilliantined prime.

Like other retired players, I adopted umpiring.

It is the funniest of games. Umpiring for *Punch* last summer (and 'for' is the right preposition), Richard Gordon, wearing an

MCC blazer and boater, insisted on standing at right-angles to the bowler's wicket, in order, he said, to see no-balls more easily. When the opposition were batting this eccentric stance did not inhibit his finger from shooting up if a fielder so much as coughed. Terrible retribution awaits us this summer.

So wrote the Literary Editor of *The Times*, who was making up the *Punch* side.

This is starkly libellous.

A strong-minded man might decorate himself with a florid tomato omelette MCC blazer. No considerate one would top it with the matchingly vivid hatband. Mine was of the Garrick Club, salmon and cucumber slices.

Anyway, doctors often do put their finger up when people cough.

I remain puzzled by the elegant reprimand. As Peter May once instructed me, 'You never criticize the umpire if you win.'

Now I play cricket only on Boxing Day. We hammer stumps into the frozen lawn at Bromley, spread cochineal on the snow for creases, and play an involved family game with everyone on both sides and a jug of Black Velvet positioned at square-leg.

I was aged 54 when first picked for Kent.

A cricket correspondent of *The Times* was once reminded by Colin Cowdrey at Canterbury, 'of the time P. F. Warner, aged about 60, was batting in the nets in a sun-hat and a pundit, observing from behind, said: "Who is that youngster? He shapes uncommonly well".'

I took an early bed the night before, wondering excitedly if I should cut the same figure.

The day of the match dawned. It was raining.

It rained all day.

'Don't worry,' Colin had already assured me earnestly, 'you'll field first slip, I'll take everything coming to your right and Knotty'll take everything coming to your left, and you won't have to bat, I'll declare — even if that loses the game by one run.'

Kent were playing our local cricket club for Derek Underwood's benefit year.

It was still raining as darkness fell. I never took the field. But in the pavilion that night I danced with Mrs Underwood, who is lovely.

Opening
Partnership

CRICKETERS' WIVES ARE young, pretty and chatty. The happiest have not the slightest interest in cricket. The saddest dare not show themselves in the shops when hubby makes a duck.

Cricketing marriages are seldom declared. The game induces such placidity and steadfastness, so temperate a response to misfortune, such resolution against personal plight, so much self-discipline and so little self-pity, the National Marriage Council should scatter in pairs tickets for Lord's.

Or perhaps cricketers are such talented marital all-rounders their wives never hanker for the next man in.

My wife knew of my cricketophilia before the vicar called, 'Play!' She was my assistant at Oxford in the Faculty of Anaesthetics created by Lord Nuffield — famous for his generous donations to medicine, less for his free sanitary towels to the women's services in the Second World War.

I asked her to marry me because she sportingly did my work while I watched cricket in the Parks, the lovely ground under the windows of the University Pathology Department where in 1940 Professor Howard Florey discovered penicillin.

Professor Alexander Fleming, of St Mary's Hospital at

Paddington in London, discovered that penicillin mould did funny things to staphylococci germs in 1928, but did nothing much about it. Dreadful arguments arose about who should get the knighthoods and Nobel Prizes.

In the end they went halves. Oxford's Edwardian Professor of Medicine Sir William Osler had already made the point: 'In science the credit goes to the man who convinces the world, not the man to whom the idea first occurs,' but the row between Paddington and the Parks continued with such biting academic ferocity I could write a novel about it in 1977.

The Parks and pathology were intimately related. 'Professor Dreyer', wrote Florey's biographer of Florey's predecessor in the Chair, 'was known for his work on syphilis, and one of the College Fellows spoke earnestly of the dangers of allowing him to keep his animals in a building adjoining the University Parks. Syphilitic goats, he predicted, would escape and infect innocent members of the University during their recreations.'

What a terrible thing for a young man to inform his doctor, 'I got it fielding at long-leg from a goat.'

The Editor of *Punch* Alan Coren, and myself, may debatably be professional humorists but are undeniably the only pair ever both married to anaesthetists. Dr Coren is a consultant at a London hospital. Literature occasionally shares a bed with medicine.

Dazzling Dr Miriam Stoppard on TV is married to a playwright.

An author's life is lovely. You need never go out if it is raining.

'Any young lady can write a book who has a sufficiency of pens and paper,' Anthony Trollope listed the advantages. 'It can be done anywhere; in any clothes. Who else is free of all shackle as to hours? The Prime Minister must be in his place on that weary front bench shortly after prayers, and must sit there, either asleep or awake. The author may do his work at five in the morning when he is fresh from his bed, or at three in the morning before he goes there.'

I am an averagely prolific author, which means only that I am a man of averagely sedentary habits. As C. S. 'Hornblower' Forester, who had leg trouble, reminded me, it is one of the two professions which can be performed lying on your back.

Research is essential steelwork in the construction of the modern novel. Thackeray and P. G. Wodehouse never did research. *I* must, or risk publisher's eyebrow-raising for carelessness and irresponsibility.

I always do it after the book is written, as more restful.

After the penicillin novel, I leisurely researched in Cologne about Professor Domagk, whose discovery gave Florey the idea of anti-bacterial wonder-drugs — the sulpha group, which first benefited the world in the winter of 1933, a month before Hitler blighted it. Finishing a novel about the invention of anaesthesia brought an unhurried week in Boston researching the Ether Dome atop the Massachusetts General Hospital, where 'etherization' was first performed in 1846 (the frock-coated doctors who clapped the miracle were severely shushed by the surgeon — 'Applause is not proper in the operating room').

A novel about Florence Nightingale provided more than a delightful lazy holiday at Istanbul. She is a woman in my life. She is a woman in every doctor's life. Miss Nightingale found nursing a rough trade and left it a fine art. Her teaching put her imprint on every living nurse, like St Peter's finger-marks on haddock.

Her four-towered Scutari hospital still stands across the Bosporous like an upturned billiard-table. The barrack-rooms are bright and warm and smelling of soldiers' lunch, and polished plastic now tiles the four miles of floors on which a British Army died.

I had lived so long in the pictures of the *Illustrated London News* I had the stirring feeling of being Miss Nightingale's ghost, with soldiers kissing my passing shadow thrown by The Lamp.

This was not the Aladdin sort Miss Nightingale extends towards the Athenaeum Club in Waterloo Place and which illuminates our £10 notes. She used a collapsible linen Turkish Army one, like a Chinese lantern holding a candle. It throws insufficient light to kiss anything with. I know this because the Nightingale Nurses invited me to St Thomas's Hospital, and after dinner turned the lights out and lit it.

Miss Nightingale was a woman composed of common sense, adaptability, endurance, unpretentiousness, grace, intelligence, determination and humour. She is a woman of whom our country is rightly proud, because she could have come from no other.

She was called Florence because her mother happened to be there at the time, during her long Italian tour. She could have been Pisa Nightingale or Venice Nightingale or Leghorn Nightingale. 'She was a shocking nurse,' decided her sister Parthenope (Greek for Naples, which Mrs Nightingale had reached earlier). Parthenope knew, Florence having ruthlessly nursed her from childhood.

Florence Nightingale did none of the dirty work at Scutari, which was done by the dirty nurses. She raised money like a pop star in a famine and terrorized the hidebound Army doctors because no one knew how to court-martial her. This when women's liberation was restricted to unknotting the stays after fainting.

A tough administrator, a cunning politician, Miss Nightingale would today be in the Cabinet. Or make a sweet-running machine of our ramshackle National Health Service, more wonderously.

She was also les.

When a gentleman fell in love with her at 23, she fell in love with his sister. She was in love with the tousled-haired tomboy 'Clarkey' and also with the Dean of Westminster's sister —

31

until she unexpectedly appeared in Constantinople with a rival bunch of nurses.

'I do believe I am "like a man", as Parthe says,' Florence wrote to Clarkey. 'And my experience of women is almost as large as Europe. And it is so intimate too. I have lived and slept in the same bed with English Countesses and Prussian Bauerinnen .... No woman has excited "passion" among women more than I have.'

Being then 41, and being Florence Nightingale, she presumably meant what she said.

This was a small part of the novel but a big part of anything about it in the Sunday papers. On the Monday morning I was to publicize its publication at Miss Nightingale's St Thomas's Hospital. I arrived to discover the publicity man outside, ashen-faced.

'It's all off,' he gasped. 'The Press Conference. The Matron has just told me. What on earth do we do?'

I replied simply, from experience: 'Nothing. When a Matron says something's off, it stays off.'

We met the Press instead under Florence Nightingale's statue, and, as only the *Sun* and *The Times* showed up, achieved the limits of journalistic opinion.

Only once have I taken the 1930s advice, 'The best novels are written in cheap hotel bedrooms in the south of France,' and torn myself from Bromley. In the winter of 1957 I took an expensive hotel bedroom in Torremolinos, a word which had not yet entered the English language.

Over my first Fundador the barman exclaimed, 'Oh, there is another English doctor staying in the hotel! You will be able to have many interesting conversations. Let me see — ' He rustled the list of guests. 'Dr John Bodkin Adams.'

Dr Adams had recently been acquitted at the Old Bailey of murdering a patient for a legacy, suspected of murdering a hundred more, then struck off the medical *Register* for such

32

unalarming crimes as botching cremation certificates and prescribing his private patients NHS elastic stockings.

Bodkin Adams was a broken man. This did not seem to worry him in the slightest. A short, fat, talkative, jovial fellow in a trilby which turned up all the way round, he busily organized rubbers of bridge with the English widows staying at the hotel, who adored him.

We did not have that interesting conversation. I did not know how to start, apart from, 'Read any good wills recently?'

A woman whose husband abruptly turns author needs devote herself to his household wants 24 hours a day, but is exalted into an Aeolian harp singing in his winds of inspiration. Hers is the privilege of hearing from his morning tea to nightcap — sometimes when urgently woken during the night — his wonderful new fantasies. Her soul feels the agonies of his during their processing for the public. At last she can read through his thick manuscript at one go (without yawning).

My wife gamely stuck this for 30 years before she declared she preferred a return to anaesthetics in middle-age rather than face the thirty-first.

I felt her decision was coloured by the Cricket Whistle.

Summer Saturday television becomes infuriatingly interrupted by show-jumping (why cannot they build the fences lower, then they would not keep getting knocked over?) and running ('I can think of no entertainment that fills me with greater detestation than a display of competitive athletics, none — except possibly folk-dancing,' said Evelyn Waugh, rightly).

I bought a ref's whistle and invited her to sit in front of the set, recalling me urgently from the garden once sanity returned with the Test Match.

She refused to play.

So I started as a doctor, became an author and ended as a Bromley housewife.

Every morning I wave goodbye in my night-clothes to the family cake-winner. I shut the front door. I am alone in our Edwardian villa with the dog.

All round doors slam, cars start, the suburban tide goes out. Each house left silent holds The Captive Wife, which sociologists write books about.

I make my breakfast at the kitchen sink.

Like all doctors, I am a rabid hypochondriac. I recoil from butter, eggs, milk as from an asp discovered in the fridge. Wholemeal bread smeared with Gentleman's Relish seems pretty safe.

Housework is a doddle. I have no sympathy with brow-clasping housewives expressing preference for slavery in Siberian salt-mines. I make the bed, feed the dog, puff up the cushions, charge the dishwasher, shake the mat. It takes ten minutes. The rest of the day being my own, I have developed the characteristics of Bromley housewives.

I hold endless telephone conversations with my friends. I talk back to the radio. I fly to the nylon net at the faintest disturbance to our suburban serenity outside. I store up interesting items like the dog being sick or the poinsettia wilting to swap later for my wife's cares of the day. I exchange family histories with the postman and the men come to read the meters. If we had a milkmaid instead of a milkman, God knows what would happen.

Like all Bromley housewives I am careful about my figure.

At one o'clock I have my diet — a lettuce leaf with grated carrot at the kitchen formica. The unnoticably brief meal finished, I recall a side of smoked salmon handy in the fridge, and feel dietetically justified in adding a slice or two. Smoked salmon traditionally demands buttered brown bread, also a glass or so of cold Chablis '84 from the cellar.

I begin to remember substantial left-overs of last night's *boeuf à la bourguignonne* with *pommes Dauphine*. This is speedily heated by the miracles of modern microwaves and necessitates a bottle of Chateau Margaux '72.

Then there is the fruit salad with Grand Marnier to be finished up, and the crumbling Stilton will hardly wait another meal, all needing washing down with a glass or so of Croft's '66, and I lie flat out on the sofa until my wife gets home for her dinner.

Nowadays I must cut my own sandwiches before cricket, gut my own trout after fishing, and read the medical journals to keep up with domestic conversation. I reckon I deserve on all three counts Rex Harrison's compliment to Robert Morley — 'He said I had the right sort of life. "One house, one wife, and, if you will forgive me saying so, Robert, one performance".'

French Cricket

I INTRODUCED CRICKET INTO France for the season of 1937.

I was not the first cricketer with the idea.

'Where now shall we match the enthusiasm of the Earl of Dorset, who carried his zeal for cricket to the Embassy at Paris, and would have encountered eleven of his country-men on French soil, had not the revolution intervened?' wondered John Nyren, the John Arlott of the Men of Hambledon.

The 38-year-old 3rd Duke had arrived as ambassador to Paris in 1783. How typically perverse of the French to ruin an Englishman's seemly enjoyment by holding a revolution.

Particularly as the French Revolution stands in the history books only through absence of cricket.

'If the French aristocrats had played cricket with their peasants, their chateaux would not have been burnt,' judged George Macaulay Trevelyan, Master of Trinity.

How much more civilized, more English, had the Paris streets rung not with the cry, 'A la lanterne!' but become plastered with posters:

AVIS!

GRAND MATCH OF CRICKET — FOR THE FUTURE OF
FRANCE!

Place de Grève — 14 July 1789

THE ARISTOCRATS XI

(Capt. Louis XVI)

υ

THE SANS-CULOTTES

(Capt. Danton, G-J.)

Adequate parking for tumbrels.

Luncheon by Maxim's.

The losing side will be guillotined at the close of play.

Cricket may have French blood.

My fellow doctor-writer Emile Littré was clearly also an enthusiast for *criquet*, defined in his 1863 *Dictionnaire de la langue française* as *jeu d'adresse*, a game of skill. In 1881 Frédéric Godefroy's *Dictionnaire de l'ancienne langue française et tous ses dialectes du IXe au XVe siècle* gives *criquet* for a stick used as the target in a bowling-alley, and mentions a petitioner leaving the Château de Liettes near St Omer in 1478 — 70 years before our Guildford schoolboys — and wandering where they bowled at a vine-stake or *criquet*.

Or cricket may have started as Flemish *krick*, which is either a prop or the gallows.

Philologists argue endlessly about this all over Europe.

Cricket rooted better in Belgium. The Burgomaster of Brussels declared open a cricket ground in the Valley of the English amid the nearby woods 50 years after Waterloo, and they were still playing until the Second World War.

It flourished among the tulips. The land of Felix is a member (second-class) of the International Cricket Conference, and

38

there are somehow chilling photographs of The Hague Cricket Club in flannels during the Nazi occupation.

France, through the versatile Huguenots, made a lasting contribution to cricket:

> At home, one has to note, it was a Bosanquet who gave to cricket, a game that might have been devised in order to be incomprehensible to the French, the invention of the googly; and so introduced a streak of deception into its early innocence. That is a subject for meditation in itself.

Expect *The Times* to mix gratitude and condescension when talking to foreigners.

Like the cast of Terence Rattigan's *French Without Tears*, I was sent to a Paris school to learn French.

I had automatically packed my cricket bat and ball, objects eyed with the curiosity, qualms and amusement aroused by Amazonian explorers' shrunken heads.

Teaching French was by permitting no foreign languages at meals. If you did not speak French you did not eat. The simple repast of *potage de légumes*, a *baguette*, and *ragoût de boeuf* so transcended the English boarding-school's shepherd's pie and currant duff I was a quick learner.

Soon I had chalked three stumps on the brick wall of the dusty playground and was positioning my schoolmates at *courte-jambe, long-sur et dans le ravin*, puzzling the authorities with their concerted shouts of '*Comment ça?*' like those spoilsport revolutionaries' '*Ca-ira!*'

If it never caught on in France, neither did Guinness.

That was the summer of the Great Exposition to promote peace in Europe, German and Russian pavilions glaring at each other through the feet of the Eiffel Tower. Then all of Europe was far-away countries inhabited by people of whom we knew as little as the one which drew us to war. The emetic

Channel was an encouragement to lazy isolationism, crossed only by the rich or the inquisitive. The self-contained European nations were still unhomogenized by American cult and culture.

France had different clothes, cigarettes, buses, films, telephones and street-lights from anywhere else. And different smells — the first whiff of coffee, garlic, the Metro, the *vespacienne* street gents' where passers-by could see your feet as you did it — were unforgettable.

Evelyn Waugh discerned, 'At the age of thirty-five one needs to go to the moon, or some such place, to recapture the excitement with which one first landed at Calais,' when his alternative was still fantastic.

Toubib being slang for doctor, *Doctor in the House* inevitably appeared as *Toubib or not Toubib.*

It did as sadly as cricket.

But it had me appear on the most entertaining chat show ever televised. Another guest in the Paris studio was a bee-keeper, who brought his bees, who escaped in the middle of the programme.

The French, being a nation of intellectuals, read only literature which wins literary prizes. I shall never achieve the Prix Goncourt (which is only 50 francs, but you get a free lunch at the excellent Restaurant Drouant).

In England, I won the Whitbread Prize.

The British public is not in the slightest interested in books. They are dreary items. You have to *read* them. Not even pictures, as Alice noticed.

The British public is intemperately interested in cricket, football, the races. 'Sport is the music of the Englishman,' a Danish professor told us.

Thus the Booker Prize glitters among the glories of English Literature. Television close-ups of the hopeful heaving bosoms of tarted-up lady authors and the frilly dress-shirt-fronts of the publishers combine the genteel culture of the

Sunday papers with the raucous excitement of the Grand National.

The champagne pops, and the sales of the winning novel, like those of the Fr 50 Goncourt, intoxicatingly hit the empty stomach of the book trade.

Arousing publicity for books is otherwise as difficult as turning Rodin's *Thinker* into a blood donor. The National Book League mysteriously once tried pushing sales by filling bookshop windows with large photographs of writers, overlooking P. G. Wodehouse's discovery: 'Authors without exception look like something that would be passed over with a disdainful jerk of the beak by the least fastidious buzzard in the Gobi Desert.'

Readers' psychology is odd. It should be assiduously taught by university departments of creative writing and writers-in-residence everywhere.

Readers never read the books they buy. To take the literary prize home makes them feel intellectual, as selecting from the shop's dominating shelves a book on dieting makes them feel slim, cookery books make them feel gourmets, and sex guides make them sexy.

If everyone read our annual output of books, we should be a nation of cultured, emaciated, randy Mrs Beetons.

Readers never buy the books they read. They are all women. With famous female self-sacrifice they endure the fag of visiting the public library, the irksomeness of squinting along the shelves, the tedium of the waiting-list, the snootiness of the librarians, the risk of fines, to share at last with the author the printed page with the sighing voluptuousness of the marriage bed, for which I get 0.92p a go.

I won the Whitbread Prize in the mid-1940s.

Whitbreads were generous towards Bart's Hospital. We at Bart's Hospital drank generous amounts of Whitbreads' beer, brewed round the corner in Chiswell Street. It was a sensible working relationship.

Every Christmas Whitbreads generously invited the Bart's housemen and senior students to an afternoon tour of the brewery. We were courteously greeted in the cobbled courtyard of the historic building, with its Suffolk punches and massive drays, by a monocled director who led us towards the vast brick brew-houses holding the foaming vats.

Students not invited before wondered nervously if they were really having to tour the bloody brewery. More experienced members of the profession knew that at the main entrance the courteous director would abruptly stop, turn and mention as an afterthought, 'But I expect you doctors would like to look into the sampling-room first?'

The underground sampling-room contained free-flowing samples of every beer Whitbreads made, including the brew exclusively for our monocled director and his friends.

After the tour Whitbreads generously provided a splendid tea, with muffins, currant cake, trifle, cream buns, jam tarts. As we had passed the whole afternoon in the sampling-room, few ever made the tea. The Whitbread Prize of a beer-mug was awarded to anyone who did. Two of us shared it. I was sick afterwards. I promise not to be if they give me the literary one.

I usually squeeze in my holiday between the fourth and the Oval Tests, fishing at Llawrfaennenogstumdwy (which is in Wales).

When my wife insisted on obtaining culture instead from the châteaux of the Loire, I complied. Culture is most agreeably obtained by inspecting French classical architecture while noticing it is getting on for lunch.

Though avoiding the *nouvelle cuisine*, France's greatest mistake since the Vichy Government. Serving glass domes, as once preserved British Rail sandwiches on buffet counters, displaying tiny scraps of colourful food artistically arrayed only makes Picasso a great cook. French restaurants now unbelievably *boast* of ostracizing Normandy double cream,

43

eggs and butter from their lovely sauces — why should I suffer if 55 million Frenchmen are worse hypochondriacs than I am?

Since my schooldays I have developed *Reisefieber*, journey fever. Freud's wife Martha was a sad sufferer. It obliged him to take all his holidays with her younger and jollier sister Minna instead.

I pace the deck of the Dover ferry agonizing over losing my passport and being robbed, mugged, run over by lunatic French drivers, breaking my bottle of duty-free, while our Bromley home is meanwhile burgled and razed to the ground and the dog is pining in kennels.

On the homeward ferry I was once horrified to read in the British Customs list of prohibited goods Flick knives, Counterfeit currency, Horror comics, Most animals and birds whether alive or dead (e.g., stuffed) and *Sausage*. I crammed down a foot-long *saucisson sec* in mid-Channel to avoid a jail sentence. The gold-braided Customs men, all looking as if just stepped from the bridge of *Invincible*, frighten me badly. I always feel the car boot is crammed with heroin or illegal immigrants. I sweated to recall that milk products were banned too, and it would not take a trained sniffer-dog to expose our Camembert.

I am terrified of falling ill. It is dreadful abroad, nursed by nuns and no newspapers. French institutional cooking — as a woman who need no longer take care to be beautiful becomes a slut — is vile. I shivered at George Orwell's hospital experience of *la soupe*, cabbage-tasting water floating with slimy bread (*la casserole* was the bedpan).

We had a comfortable, tucked-away hotel on the river Loire. I roused my wife at three in the morning.

'What if the hotel catches fire?' it had occurred to me.

She said what?

I outlined, 'We're on the top floor, there's no fire escape and only one set of stairs with those mingy French lights you press and have to scuttle down because they go out in five seconds.

Why, we'd be trapped! We'd be like those *crêpes Suzette* at dinner, long before the *sapeurs-pompiers* — the fire brigade — got here *ventre à terre*, split-arse.'

She asked if I was mad and went to sleep.

Next day we visited the châteaux of Chenonceaux and Azay-le-Rideau. I looked up 'Help!' in the French dictionary, to get it absolutely right. We visited the châteaux de Chambord and Blois. I decided that with châteaux, like night-clubs, once you have seen one you have seen the lot.

My *Reisefieber* became worse. I spent the evening plotting my escape. I could trapeze on a rope of knotted sheets to the dining-room balcony, abseil to the kitchen and make a soft landing in the rhododendrons.

My wife appeared for bed and inquired what I was doing.

'Knotting the sheets.'

'Yes! You *are* mad.'

I explained, 'In case of fire during the night.'

'May I make clear, I prefer being burnt alive to sleeping in those blankets? If you don't remake the bed instantly I shall go home tomorrow and you'll have to drip-dry your own shirts.'

Marriage to a lady doctor often demands diplomatic acquiescence to an incisive personality. I wonder if the Editor of *Punch* and Tom Stoppard feel the same?

Next holiday I shall pack a rope. If it is not long enough, I can avoid ante-mortem cremation by hanging myself from the wardrobe.

Luncheon Interval

If the left is serious in its aim to make us one nation, it could do worse than start by abolishing lunch. For lunch is a social divider of infinite power. It distances husbands from their wives and bosses from their workers. It is a precise gauge of the gap between the haves and the have-nots. It is the inner temple of the expense-account cult and the last bastion of the male chauvinist. It is both a perk of privilege and a symptom of decadence. No one in Shakespeare has lunch. Lunch is a new-fangled notion born of affluence and frivolity.

So wrote my luncheon companion Godfrey Smith.

A Lord's Test with no lunch would be like Christmas with no dinner.

Lunch has been a worthy decoration to the structure of cricket since the eighteenth century men of Hambledon took their dinner-hour from 2 to 3.

I love the theatre, but it does so ruin an evening. Dine before the show, you miss the second act denouement through dropping off and annoying your neighbours with your snores.

Dine after, you become inattentive to such dramatic climaxes as Cleopatra applying the asps, through thinking of a nice fillet steak with french fries and crispy onions and a bottle of the better Beaune, and annoy your neighbours with your tummy rumbles.

Glyndebourne obviates this inconvenience by breaking in the middle for dinner, which sends the audience sound asleep despite all that noise only a few feet away. I have anyway been less sensitive to the glories of Glyndebourne since the lovely June afternoon I needed quit Lord's to don a dinner-jacket and drive towards Brighton leaving May and Cowdrey at the wicket.

I had invited Dr Miles Hoxton to the Lord's Test because he promised to bring lunch and his wife was a superb cook.

This was from his fussing so about his food. Miles was a worrier. When we were students together he fretted endlessly over his exams, his thinning hair, whether his girl-friends were pregnant. He got *Reisefieber* on the bus.

He was at the Grace Gates with a hamper. He had a busy practice in north London. He was a wonderfully sympathetic doctor, because he imagined he had everything his patients got.

We settled in the sun on top of the Warner Stand. The Australians took the field.

'Richard!' It was Mr Basil Brassfoal QC, a big booming barrister. 'Room for a small one to squeeze in?'

He separated Miles and myself like an elephant in long grass.

'I suppose you doctors have been pondering on Sideaway v Bethlem Royal Hospital *et alii*?' Basil asked heartily as I introduced Miles.

I inquired confusedly where the fixture had been played.

Basil laughed loudly. 'Not Lord's but the House of. The Law Lords have decided that every doctor must tell every patient absolutely everything about all possible complications, so the patient can assess the risks before consenting to treatment. Didn't you see it in the papers?'

I pronounced, 'What lordly lunacy. Most patients can't even follow the directions on the label for taking the pills.'

47

Basil chuckled, shaking shoulders like kerbstones. 'That's what I like to hear from your doctors! Just carry on regardless. Lots of lovely malpractice suits. How I love my work — it combines the craftiness of snooker, the cunning of chess, the guile of fly-fishing, the subtle penalty-provoking of rugger and the decorum of cricket. I say! Flashing outside the off stump in the first over. At this rate we'll be all out by lunch.'

Miles was suddenly looking nervous. 'You must share ours,' he mumbled.

'How very kind,' Mr Basil Brassfoal QC accepted zestfully.

He declared he must have a pee, which the Warner Stand contrives gentlemen to perform without missing the cricket. I remember thus watching Frank Worrell bowled for a duck by Fred Trueman in the 1963 Test which Colin Cowdrey saved by batting with a fractured left arm.

Miles grabbed my elbow.

'I had a patient at morning surgery. He's here at the match. Young salesman, name of Javetts. Luxury kitchens, lots of money in it, he says you can measure a husband's guilt over his mistress by what he spends on the wife's kitchen. Right inguinal hernia. Advised operation. Consultation over in five minutes. Never mentioned complications.'

Miles gripped the edge of his seat.

'Might all come apart at the seams afterwards. Get infected — filthy places, hospitals, everyone bringing their germs with them. End with nasty uggy mass up his trousers.' He cried agonizedly, 'The spermatic cord! It runs through the operation site like a power cable through roadworks. Slightest slip, he'll end up with only one ball.'

'Why worry?' I consoled him cheerfully. 'One's enough, Nature thoughtfully packed a spare. Howzat? He's out!'

'I don't think I can take much interest in the cricket,' Miles said miserably.

Our lunch was shrimps shawled in smoked salmon, juicy cold steak-and-kidney pie, strawberries and cream, and

49

Bollinger. Mr Basil Brassfoal QC, like Gilbert and Sullivan's Judge, had an appetite keen and hearty.

He promised to bring the lunch tomorrow.

Miles appeared with the hamper again. He mentioned that his wife had split the pair of lobsters and cracked the claws.

'How's your hernia patient?' I asked, as we found seats.

He gulped. 'I phoned him. I'd remembered other things. Front teeth knocked out by hamfisted anaesthetist. Burns from surgeon's electric cautery. Paralysis from being put on the operating table wrong way round. How can a GP *know* all the complications?' he complained crossly. 'Particularly as these days they seem to be invented hourly. He asked where he could buy a truss.'

The Australian openers reached the wicket.

'Then I remembered Mrs Noon,' Miles continued agitatedly. 'Gall-bladder. Awaiting operation. I phoned to say the surgeon might cut the wrong bit — happen to anyone, even Prime Ministers, poor Anthony Eden's bile-duct gave him more problems than the Suez Canal. And she might go out like a light afterwards from a clot hitting her lung, or more lingeringly from some ghastly pulmonary infection.'

'Did she die of fright?'

'She laughed. Said if she worried about the pilot she'd never get to Majorca for her holidays, and anyway you doctors are wonderful.'

We laid out lunch in the Coronation Garden. Mr Basil Brassfoal QC jumped the low wall, apologizing cheerfully he had been kept too long in chambers to nip into Fortnum's.

'Lobsters!' His eyes glistened. He had the obsession about food of the Three Men in a Boat. 'Dreadfully sad they're so expensive. But how very kind! I'd love one.'

Saturday morning. The first innings scores were nearly equal. We savoured a fascinating day.

'I could hardly sleep,' Miles greeted me unhappily. 'Mrs Noon's complications. The anaesthetics might explode and wreck the theatre, if not the entire hospital. She could catch those diseases always lurking round the wards — food-poisoning, legionnaires, AIDS I shouldn't be surprised. And patients fall out of bed, get multiple fractures. But she said she might escape it all by being struck by lightning on the way in.'

'You've gashed your forehead.'

'I hit the windscreen.'

'But how?' I asked solicitously.

'When the bus rammed the back of my car.'

'Oh, I'm sorry.'

'I stopped rather suddenly in Wellington Road. I saw a phone box. The cats.'

'Cats?'

'NHS hospitals. Infested with feral cats, I remembered. Mr Javetts could catch cat-scratch fever, very painful. Rats!' he exclaimed. 'Lots in hospital kitchens, dreadful disgrace. Easily get rat bites.'

He dabbed rapidly at his cut with a swab.

'Human bites! Many hospital patients suddenly go berserk. Why, the whole place might collapse about him! Always happening to the NHS, remember the 8 million quid extension to the famous Children's Hospital, had to be closed instantly because it started dropping into Great Ormond Street.'

I was curious how the patient had responded.

'Said the hernia was disappearing under his eyes, must be a hallucination, further had no more intention of seeing the inside of a hospital than of those atomic piles at Sellafield.'

Miles staggered with the hamper. Lunch was cold poussin with tarragon stuffing and he had brought enough for four.

After the first over he leapt up.

'Mrs Noon! Patients often get muddled up. She could end with the wrong operation. Where's a phone-box?'

He missed two wickets.

I asked when he returned, 'Did she take warning?'

'She said she didn't care if she got mixed with a maternity case and went home with sextuplets.'

In the Coronation Garden we opened the hamper and the claret.

'Look!' Miles's jaw dropped. 'My hernia with your barrister. Sueing me before he's even had the operation. A bit sharp, even for the law.'

'My dear doctor,' Mr Basil Brassfoal greeted him jovially. 'Met one of your patients in the champagne tent. Last month he sold me a magnificently luxurious kitchen for my wife. I was glad to put his mind at rest about his operation.'

The curly-haired young man in a blue blazer grinned.

'Can't wait, doctor. Mr Brassfoal says it's perfectly safe because the slightest slip will bankrupt the surgeon. And the going rate for losing one of my whatnots would save me the sweat of selling luxury kitchens for the rest of my life.'

'So we must hope that the operation will prove entirely unsuccessful,' I suggested.

'Beychevelle '72!' Mr Basil Brassfoal QC rubbed his hands and eyed the bottle. 'An excellent year. I'm laying down quite a decent little cellar, courtesy of you bungling doctors.'

'How's the girl-friend?' I asked him quietly.

He paled.

'I am not prepared to answer leading questions.'

Mr Basil Brassfoal QC bit into his chicken. He made no more disparaging remarks about doctors for the rest of the match.

Australia won.

The Cricketing Doctor

A T THE TOP OF THE northernmost vast staircase in Lord's pavilion hangs a small cartoon by 'the incomparable Max' Beerbohm glorifying the bulky embodiment of cricket, huge feet splayed, beard like a bunch of grapes, handwritten in the corner, 'Portrait of dear old W.G. — to the left is the grandstand; to the right, the funeral of one of his patients.'

A four-plumed hearse with a black horse leads a carriage of mourners with a crêpe-hatbanded driver.

This is a slur. Dr W. G. Grace enjoyed a low mortality-rate. He attended so few patients.

Better than Herbert Farjeon's girl who danced with a man, who's danced with a girl, who's danced with the Prince of Wales, I watched cricket with a man who watched W. G. Grace.

'W. G. Grace and G. K. Chesterton were two big men with tiny voices,' Ben Travers enlightened me at Lord's during the Gillette Cup Final of 1972. 'And you know, Grace always had his bat a foot in the air when the bowler bowled to him.'

England's veteran spinner of farce, from *A Cuckoo in the Nest* in 1925 to *The Bed Before Yesterday* in 1975, was born when W. G. Grace was 38 and had an off season with the bat — 1,846 runs averaging 35.50 — but a good one with the ball, 122 wickets at 19.99 apiece.

As a Charterhouse schoolboy Ben Travers could see W.G. averaging 23.40 and taking 20 for 482. As a 20-year-old he could still see W.G. making 241 runs with an average of 26.77 and taking 13 wickets at 20.61.

I unexpectedly met Ben standing on the coach mound at Lord's, where once you watched from the top of your carriage over the Warner Stand's precursor. It was during England v West Indies in 1966, when Sobers and Holford had a record sixth-wicket partnership of 274, leaving England to make 284 in 240 minutes (we failed).

I was speechless. It was like finding myself next to Chaucer when Kent were playing at Canterbury. I stammered something about him being my mentor. 'Mentor my arse,' said Ben, I felt promising a rewarding acquaintanceship.

Ben Travers was responsible for our retaining the Ashes in 1956. When a Royal Naval Air Service instructor during the First World War, he trained Sub-Lt. May to fly and claimed that had he skimped the job Peter would never have been fathered to become England's captain.

At 64 Ben wrote that, 'Volumes and volumes of elderly Wisdens bear still my fingerprints in chocolate upon the pages.' Age could not wither the infinite variety of his humour. Over 90, he told on television the appealing story of a yachting friend desirous to be buried at sea, a production that failed because they had forgotten to drill holes in the coffin. Ben thought he was still drifting round the world.

He retired at 85 to Rye, a resort swept by literary breezes on the Sussex coast, where Henry James and E. F. Benson wrote such different novels gazing from the same window down the cobbled steep street towards the Mermaid Inn. He shortly returned to London, finding it too dull in the evenings.

'Never resent growing old,' said Maurice Chevalier. 'Think of the many who are denied the privilege.'

Or as ex-Prime Minister Attlee put it, on being asked how it felt to be 80: 'Wonderful, compared with the alternative.'

Ben wrote on 10 August 1980:

If you're very old and you're a writer like me, you know that you only have a short time to live, so if you still have things to write about you mustn't waste your time. And if you've a reputation and you want to keep it, you have to be more and more careful that what you do is up to scratch. My wastepaper baskets in their lifetime have seen 90 per cent of what I've written. I think about death a great deal — almost all the time, but then anyone of my age would. Each morning you open your eyes and think, what, again?

Four months later he did not, and the public stock of harmless pleasure was impoverished as by the death of the genius of the club he embellished.

I was admitted myself to the Garrick Club shortly after *Dixon of Dock Green* Ted Willis had enlivened *Doctor in the House* for the stage. It opened in Morecambe, on a New Year's Day so cold they were landing the famous prawns ready deep-frozen. It has since appeared on many piers, an excuse drawing me into the seemly sybaritism of our summer resorts.

The play opens with the stage manager nervously imparting through the curtains that the leading lady has suffered an accident, and 'Is there a doctor in the house?'

This cues the two leading men to shout from opposite sides of the auditorium, 'I am a doctor!' The effect is sometimes spoiled by a zealous GP, possibly excited like Dr Johnson by the white bosoms of our actresses, getting in first and clambering on to the stage.

I cannot trace who first issued across the footlights this invitation on which I have lived a comfortable life and raised a family. The most likely performance occurred at Ford's Theatre, Washington on 14 April 1865, but I learned from *The Times* disappointingly: 'There was a rush towards the President's box, when cries were heard of "Stand back and give him air. Has anyone stimulants?"'

It is a cry always upstaging the drama being performed. Ralph Richardson once reared suddenly from an audience, crying anguishedly: 'Is there a doctor in the house?' One rose instantly from his seat. Ralph Richardson bellowed across the stalls; 'I say, doctor, isn't this a *frightful* play?'

In the 1820s Henry Mills Grace was up from Somerset to the combined medical schools of St Thomas's and Guy's. Like a useful cricketing colt, he caught the eye of the senior surgical pro Astley Cooper, who made £15,000 a year, and his footman Charles £600 in bribes for queue-jumping, and who took a lump from George IV's head and won a title.

Dr Henry Grace spurned a fashionable London practice. It would interfere with his cricket and hunting in Gloucestershire. He put up his plate at Downend, a village lying between Bristol, Thornbury and Chipping Sodbury.

Cricket was then rather vulgar, like cock-fighting. You shouted at it and bet on it. Sometimes with confidence — 'Get out of my sight, or baronet as you are, I am sure I shall be knocking you down.' Thus Alfred Mynn refused an offer to sell a match.

Dr Henry Grace's eldest son Henry became a doctor at 17 by apprenticeship to his father. That was before the Medical Act of 1858 required doctors to be educated. He became medical officer of Bristol workhouse. His second son Alfred became medical officer of Chipping Sodbury workhouse. His third son Edward became medical officer of Thornbury workhouse.

It is heartwarming for a cricket-mad doctor to discover a son's developing interest in medicine paralleled with that in his favourite game. (My pair admit grudgingly, 'You may have given us a rotten childhood, dad, but at least you put us up for MCC'.)

At 21 Edward Grace was the most famous cricketer in the

Kingdom. For MCC v Gentlemen of Kent he scored 192 not out, and took all ten wickets for the first of 31 times. Next year he went to Australia with George Parr. He was also the West Gloucester Coroner (said to be the profession of men who have failed in the two careers of medicine and the law). The cries of 'Come on, Coroner!' were never again repeated from the public benches.

W.G. Grace matured too late to enter the medical establishment through the apprentice's door. He faced the tedium of exams. He was better at cricket.

W.G. studied at Bristol Medical School, at the Westminster Hospital, then honoured my own, Bart's. Either Bart's had the most brilliant medical school in London or was as brilliant as in my day at getting us thick-witted students through. W.G. Grace qualified MRCS (England), LRCP (Edinburgh), the soft academic option, in 1879.

He was then aged 31, and that season had a batting average of 52.53 and took 919 wickets. The public was so delighted they subscribed the new doctor £1,500, a clock and two bronze ornaments.

His younger brother George, who was called Fred, had meanwhile lost repeatedly against the examiners, though playing regularly for the Gentlemen v Players at Lord's since aged 19, and at 23 scoring 165 not out for Gloucester against Yorkshire. He was keen. One morning he left at dawn for South Wales, shot 10 brace of grouse, and returned to Gloucestershire in time to score a century for the county.

Though unflinching against the quickies on a bumping pitch and a blinding light, he flattered his examiners with terror.

'My brother G. F. Grace is coming up for his surgery exam this week,' W.G. wrote from Bristol with the familiarity usually unavailable towards the examiner who has just passed you yourself. 'He has been reading at St Bartholomew's for the last few months, so is pretty well up to the mark, but he is so nervous about this exam I do not know how he will get on.

'If you can manage to get him an early number for his viva voce I shall be very glad, as it will save him waiting about and a good deal of funk. You will be glad to hear I have started in practice here, and have had between 700 and 800 fresh patients since January 1st. Unfortunately they do not all pay. Hoping you are in good health, and with kind regards.'

Even Bart's could not do miracles twice.

W.G. and the Coroner opened for England under Lord Harris against Australia in early September 1880. Fred went in No 9 and bagged a pair. He was dead before the year was out, from pneumonia blamed unjustly on a damp hotel bed.

W.G. was the parish doctor. He resembled his mother, except of course for the beard, which he started to grow at 17. He had the James Robertson Justice bedside manner, stolid, bluff, energetic, jovial, sporadically tetchy. He had hairy arms and shook hands crushingly. He was good at beagling and bowls. His catches included a fleeing pickpocket on a Gloucestershire railway station.

He took a large Scotch and soda with a dash of angostura during the luncheon interval and another at close of play. He liked his champagne properly cooled, greeting dinner guests reassuringly at his country house: 'It's all right, it's down the well.' He was a non-smoker, a doctor perceiving a century before others that: 'You can get rid of drink, but you can never get rid of smoke.'

When he came to the wicket at Lord's, 'The clubs emptied and a stream of cabs dashed towards St John's Wood.' They ran excursion trains to watch him play. When he attended evensong in Marlborough chapel, after a boy had bowled him for 3 when he had backed himself for a century, they had Hymn No 28, including,

The scanty triumphs grace hath won,
The broken vow, the frequent fall,

and the school fell about.

Such activity demanded the employment of two locums for half the year, for a whole one when W.G. was in Australia with the Earl of Sheffield of the Shield. His clinical work is skimpily recorded. He became the public vaccinator, with the interesting diagnostic ability to smell smallpox on sniffing the sufferer's bedroom.

'It is advisable for the sake of health and comfort that the cricketer should wear flannel or woollen material next to the skin,' exhibits W.G.'s grasp of contemporary medical principles. He counselled also carefully checking the size of flannels arriving from the tailor. If too small or too large, 'A revelation of this kind when you arrive on the cricket field and are getting ready to go in is destructive alike to high scoring and sweetness of temper.'

Valuable intelligence to an opposing captain, who with a stealthy switch in the dressing-room could get W.G. out cheaply by sending him to the wicket bursting from a pair of schoolboy's bags.

His most famous case was obstetrical. During Gloucester *v* Middlesex at Clifton in 1885, W.G. batted all the first day for 163, sat up all night with a patient he had promised to see through her confinement, and carried his bat on the second day for 221.

The doctor probably snatched a nap, no labour demanding constant monitoring from the drawing of stumps to the resumption of play. Unless abnormal — and perhaps it was. Dr W.G. reported to the team the next morning: 'It was fairly successful. The child died, the mother died, *but I saved the father.*'

If this was not a joke it did not much matter, if your brother is the local Coroner.

An item of Dr W.G.'s practice merits reproduction from his official *Biography*.

Grace and I were also playing together in the match, MCC and Ground *v* Nottinghamshire at Lord's in 1870, when poor

George Summers was knocked out by a fast ball from Platts the Derbyshire bowler. When this occurred, I was fielding longstop, and somehow or other I was the first to pick him up. It was an awful blow on the cheek bone. I remember W.G., who had made 117, feeling his pulse and simply remarking: 'He is not dead.' Summers was carried off insensible to the hotel on the ground, and I have always understood that he would have recovered, and his life been spared, if he would only have agreed to keep quiet. Instead of this, he would insist, quite against doctor's orders, upon coming on the ground the next day and watching the match, sitting all the time in a hot sun. After that he travelled by train to Nottingham, where he died. This tragic occurrence led to a rather humorous incident. The next man to come in to bat after Summers was knocked out was Richard Daft, who was always very dapper and rather full of self-importance. I shall never forget his coming out of the pavilion with two large towels round his head as a protection against the bowling, which was somewhat alarming at the time. I do not think I ever saw anything quite so ludicrous as was Daft's appearance at the wicket on that occasion.

Always a lot of laughs in cricket, if you don't let it kill you.

After W.G. qualified, his batting average began to drop. Nor was he the only star in the summer sky. Improved wickets brought improved batting. At 47 he enjoyed a magnificent male menopausal flush, scoring 2,346 at an average of 51.00, the first 1,000 by 30 May 1895. He claimed his hundredth hundred. Opening against Kent, he was last out for 257, then 73 not out, in the field for all the three days of the match. The public excitedly subscribed £10,000. The Press began to buzz about the Honours List. He was the Grand Old Man, the open-air Gladstone. He was known by sight better than anyone in the country. But the accolade was not then a cricketing stroke.

In 1898 Gentlemen υ Players at Lord's was switched to 18 July, his 50th birthday. Conan Doyle took only one first-class wicket, W. G. Grace's. W.G. got 83 ducks. He had one speech for cricket tour dinners: 'Gentlemen, I beg to thank you for the honour you have done me. I never saw better bowling than I have seen today and I hope to see as good wherever I go,' substituting 'batting' or 'the ground' as demanded. He thought his best innings 189 not out on the rainy day of 10 July 1871 for the Single *v* the Married, a game which has dropped from Lord's fixtures like the equally intriguing Left-handed *v* Right-handed.

W.G. played his last Test nearing 51, captaining against Australia at Trent Bridge. He made 28 and 1, and some of the crowd booed when he fumbled in the field. 'It's all over,' he muttered to F. S. Jackson on the London train. 'I shan't play again.'

After 20 years' practice he left Bristol to run the cricket at the Crystal Palace. He played his last first-class match, for the Gentlemen *v* Surrey at the Oval, in April 1908 in a snowstorm. He had made 54,896 runs and taken 2,864 wickets. He moved to Mottingham, next door to Bromley. His last game was for neighbouring Eltham *v* Grove Park in 1914. He went in No 1 and was caught for 4. The match was a draw.

His son, young W.G., played for Cambridge and died in 1905 aged 30 after an appendicectomy. He and his uncle Fred would have been spared today, sprightly George Summers, too. The oldest Grace to die was uncle Alfred at 76, the only one in the family who smoked.

The man unfrightened of bowlers like Australian Ernie Jones, who sent the ball whizzing through his whiskers, did not like the Zeppelins. You could see the bowlers, and take combative action. Early in October 1915 he had a stroke; on the 23rd he tried to get out of bed and died. He lies at Elmer's End.

W.G. was discovered never to be a registered student at Bart's. He went only for surgery cramming from Professor Howard Marsh. You still enter the W. G. Grace ward of Bart's' new Queen Elizabeth II block for your cardiac operation.

Rightly, too.

Had my hospital not scraped W.G. Grace through his finals, it would have been the loss of an extramural genius to our profession as grieving as Bacon to the law and Swift to the church.

Bad Light

GEORGE FROBISHER WAS A West Country solicitor. I met him while fishing the Dart early in the season of Queen Elizabeth II's Jubilee.

George had a face like a sunset and a waist more eloquent of local products than was the United Kingdom Dairy Association.

I wondered how he buttered up clients itching to convey their houses, make their wills and divorce their wives. When not fishing, he was beagling, stag-hunting, shooting, ferreting, butterfly-chasing, or, running out of quarry tramping round and round Dartmoor.

At dusk in The Roebuck we joyfully discovered a common fervour for cricket. A sigh ruffled George's cheerfulness like a breeze across Tor Bay. Only in cricket was Glorious Devon a minor county.

I was regrettably inflamed by scrumpy. I invited him for a day at the Jubilee Test against Australia at Lord's in June. His eyes flashed like the Eddystone Lighthouse. He had been to London only once, when one of his father's clients was hanged.

I met him at Paddington. It was a threatening cloud-ceilinged morning. He wore shooting-jacket and deerstalker and gave me a two-pound tin of clotted cream. He was boyishly excited about seeing Tommo bowl.

Londoners were arriving at Lord's with macs and umbrellas, cocking an eye skywards as warily as the summer 37 years before.

England's summer enjoyments — picnics, garden parties, school sports, vicarage fêtes, Ascot — are arranged on the lunatic assumption that the sun will be shining.

We are bleakly ungrateful to the English weather for the thrills it contributes to the English game.

Rugger and soccer pound away in the mud. At Wimbledon, the champions sulk off in the gentlest sprinkle. Only at a cricket match can an impending shower create the feverish tension which so upset Damocles.

The majestic, implacable, fickle, tantalizing weather overawes cricket like it does sailing. More subtly so — the raindrops which thud like muffled drums on one dressing-room window beat a cheerful tattoo on the other, even a darkening sky can influence the result more startlingly than a howling gale the Fastnet race.

The weather is the only ingredient of a cricket match unchanged since it rained on Broad-Halfpenny Down. Play at Fenner's stopped in April 1981 because it was too cold. At the Oval, in July 1868, Surrey v Lancashire stopped because it was too hot. An earthquake did it at Lahore in 1937. Only Shakespeare has extracted such drama so effectively from the elements.

We found seats in the Q Stand. I recalled sitting in the Father Time Stand opposite during the Australian Test of the Queen's Coronation Year, when Len Hutton as captain made 145 — a draw, but at the Oval we regained the Ashes after 19 years, Lindsay Hassett with a vanished grace putting himself on for the final over when Compo and Hutton hit the winning runs.

My gaze moved to the free seats beside the sightscreen,

where I watched with my bottle of ginger-pop the Test of her grandfather's Jubilee Year in 1935, England *v* South Africa. Then the Cape was a bit of the Empire where they shot big game and dug up diamonds, and there were white men in the West Indian team.

I sighed deeply. How pleasant to look back on my childhood, with the peculiar affection which Stephen Leacock describes everyone feels for his old school after it has been knocked down and all the masters dead long ago.

The loudspeaker overhead inquired if there was a doctor in the ground.

Faster than 'The Claw' Alan Davidson in the slips, I leapt towards the pavilion.

Since my retirement as a professional I have always been keen to play as an amateur. Any poleaxed batsman not swiftly on his feet risks my ignominious expulsion from Lord's for running headlong on the pitch.

I was soon back.

'I'd hoped that Mike Brearley would ask me to say if Bob Willis was fit to bowl,' I told George lightly. 'But it was only a kid with a cut leg on a broken beer-glass, pretty deep, though, blood all over and he'd vomited down his mother ... '

George grasped my arm. The sunset had faced from his face.

'Please!' he mumbled. 'I can pull hooks from slimy trout, I can disembowel rabbits, but I nearly faint at the *thought* of human blood.'

I apologized. The pavilion bell heralded the start of play — as at Queen Victoria's Jubilee, when watches were fewer than today's transistors.

'I'd love to be remembered for a paper in the *BMJ* on the industrial injuries of cricket,' I mused. 'A cricketer's body is his working capital, and like any other small tradesman's it's easily eroded. Left-handed John Edrich told me at the Oval he'd fractured the first bone of his right middle finger three times from the slightly short ball. The everlasting jarring on a batsman's palm can bruise right through to the back of his hand, and fast bowlers get strained lumbosacral joints because their spine flicks like a schoolboy flicking paper balls with a ruler.'

I added grimly, 'The worst injuries come from criss-crossing the country all summer. It was an accident on the road not the field which ruined Colin Milburn's sight. Umpire Hugo Yarnold died in a car crash, so did Charlie Bull of Worcester, and 18 years ago Collie Smith from Jamaica had the awful second-innings entry, "Did Not Bat Deceased".'

George had gripped my arm again.

'I nearly faint at the sight of funerals, too.'

The players took the field. It started to rain.

The unflamboyant ceremony of a cricket match pleases the English. The march of the umpires taking precedence over the spreading fielding side, the plodding rearguard batsmen, has been augmented by the Putting on of the Covers, with a dashing efficiency by the Lord's ground staff as breath-catching as the Royal Tournament.

Covers become boring to contemplate quicker than a rainy trout-stream with no fish rising.

We sat for the first of the five-and-a-half hours of the Jubilee match to be lost through rain. We ate our picnic. We moved to the Warner Stand bar.

'London weather!' grumbled George.

I apologized, having the impression that Devon, like the British Empire in my ginger-pop days, seemed never to have the sun set on it.

'Seems in for the day,' George reproached me.

I looked at my watch. Half-past three in the afternoon was, as Anthony Powell noticed, as always, a difficult time of day to deal with.

'Anywhere else you'd like to go?' I invited. 'The London Dungeon at London Bridge is a big attraction, realistic

tableaux of torture, disease and violent death through the ages.'

George grabbed my arm again.

'No, perhaps not for you,' I conceded.

'I want to visit a strip-club,' he muttered.

'Fine. I'm sure they hold matinée performances.'

Soho was full of doorways flashing GIRLS! GIRLS!! GIRLS!!! George looked far more excited than about seeing Tommo bowl.

'The permissive society?' he asked admiringly.

'I wouldn't know. I've never discovered the persons from whom the permission needed to be obtained, though plenty of national bores think themselves eligible for selection.'

He grabbed my arm.

'Not a word to the wife, if you're back fishing on the Dart. Though she'd never believe me enjoying myself except out of doors.'

'This show looks quite respectable. The foyer has house-plants.'

The box-office contained a dark-haired young man in dark glasses with drooping moustache and cigarette, clearly from the Mafia. He stared at my MCC tie.

'Still not playing, then?' he inquired interestedly. 'We've had a fair lot of them in today, with their scorecards and their sandwiches.'

We fumbled into the small, dark auditorium.

Strip-clubs operate under Rugby Union rules. When viewers leave the front row those from the second scramble into their places, those from the third taking theirs, similarly to the back row. Getting ahead of the scrum is offside, and causes much fuss.

The audience of sex-fiends resembled the carriage of any commuter train, all staring ahead with blank preoccupation. I was next to a large man in a blue blazer eyeing a naked, big-bosomed dancing girl through a hefty pair of binoculars.

He passed them to his friend with the remark in a Yorkshire accent: 'Ask me, there's definitely some swing towards the off.'

Another girl appeared and started taking off her clothes.

I grew excited.

'Look!' I hissed to George as she dangled her knickers at the audience. 'That scar across the top of her abdomen. Now I can get a good look, it's dreadfully old-fashioned. They go in a different way now, you know. To get hold of the gall-bladder and strip it off the liver with the scalpel. Less blood to mop up. I'd love to ask her where she had it done . . . '

George had seized my arm.

'Sorry!' I said. 'But this place seems more interesting than I thought.'

When the next girl removed her knickers I grasped George's arm.

'Look at that hysterectomy!' I exclaimed. 'And she can't be much over 30. Intriguing. Now that's not a bad scar at all. You'd hardly notice it unless she was stark naked in strong light. You see, they slit her down there, then retract the abdominal wall, swab the bleeding points, clamp the Fallopian tubes and oh sorry I was carried away.'

'I've had enough.' George rose. 'I should have known better than go to a strip-joint with a doctor.'

I said outside, 'It's still raining. What shall we do?'

'Go to the National Gallery. At least the nudes there will all look healthy.'

Cricket and the American Revolution

I LOVE HOLLYWOOD. It so reminds me of Bromley.

Its rectangles of neat suburban houses in pretty gardens erupt vast hotels and glittering restaurants, as though the Dorchester and Le Gavroche had replaced our British Home Stores and the local. Rodeo Drive tempts with the world's most expensive shops — diamonds, fashions, art, uniforms for your servants — all as modest as Bromley's suppliers of camping gear or pet foods. The criss-crossing streets have homely names like Brighton Way, Hillcrest Road and Elm Drive. Like Bromley, Hollywood has buses, polite policemen and a delightful cemetery.

Hollywood is famous as the home of American cricket.

In 1931 C. Aubrey Smith of Cambridge and Sussex arrived to act for MGM. He had appeared on the field with Abel and Ulyett and on the stage with Ellen Terry and Mrs Patrick Campbell. He was from Hove, a doctor's son like W. G. Grace, against whom he played. He performed for England in the first Test ever against South Africa, at Port Elizabeth, scoring 3 and taking 7. He was the captain. He was never picked again. That was in 1889. Now he was pushing 70.

Like any cricketing Englishman in outlandish surroundings he speedily established his essential sport. C. Aubrey Smith

71

was tall, heavy-browed, sweeping-moustached, pipe-smoking and left-arm medium-paced — 'Round the Corner Smith' from his run-up. Four years captaining Sussex had perfected a blunt, good-humoured, forceful, generous way of getting people to do exactly what he wanted. He soon scrambled into a team of fellow-exiles the good eggs like Ronald Colman, Errol Flynn, P. G. Wodehouse and Nigel Bruce, who batted in a brown trilby.

The first fixture of Hollywood CC was the following season of 1932, v San Fernando Valley in North Hollywood Park. Shortly Hollywood CC moved to the Fenner's of Los Angeles, the UCLA campus lying between Beverly Hills and the Ocean. In 1936 the Club, like Lord's, arrived at its third and eternal resting place. Griffith Park is near Universal Studios, where today conducted tours of their startling special effects allow you to enjoy in comfort the adventures of train smashes, armed hold-ups, typhoons and being eaten by sharks.

They rechristened it the C. Aubrey Smith Ground. They built a pav, housing a shield emblazoned with the founder's cricketing career from Charterhouse, the credits including Gentlemen v Players, and with justifiable generosity the captaincy of England v Australia in 1888, when he was only playing the lead in one of Shaw and Shrewsbury's two XIs on tour in Australia that summer. When they ceremonially opened the pavilion, Smith blubbed.

Hollywood CC produced world-famous cricketers. Sir Cedric Hardwicke, David Niven, Alan Mowbray the eternal butler, and Basil Rathbone the eternal Sherlock Holmes, Herbert Marshall, Roland Culver, Frank Lawton, Laurence Olivier, H. B. Warner who was Jesus Christ in the Cecil B. DeMille version, and George Colouris whose dream was a theatrical touring company capable of a quick-change act into a visiting cricket team, and who came home to enliven the *Doctor* movies as a peculiar patient.

Hollywood was the first cricket club to permit ladies in the pavilion, which decorated their Sunday afternoons with Olivia de Havilland, Greer Garson, Gladys Cooper, Merle Oberon and Evelyn Laye. I wonder if they made the tea.

Once in Hollywood on some business, I implored first to see the cricket ground. They stopped the studio limo, the film people withdrew — traffickers in emotions know when to leave a man to his own.

I gazed at the turf. I felt like a toiling English cleric viewing the missionary chapel radiating his faith in the heathen jungle.

With the Second World War C. Aubrey Smith did his duty. He directed the chaps to join the colours. And David Niven did. His Ground now degraded to equestrian sport would have made him shudder, like show-jumping at Lord's. He was knighted in 1944 for services to Anglo-American relations, complicated when they were winning our war and taking our money. He died four years later, aged 85.

He appeared in 100 films like *Lives of a Bengal Lancer, Little Lord Fauntleroy* and *The Prisoner of Zenda.* Also as Sir Ambrose Abercrombie, with his Eton Ramblers' blazer and I Zingari boater, the 'false and fruity' self-centred scheming stage-Englishman President of the Hollywood Cricket Club in *The Loved One* — the book.

Actors watch cricket matches with the childlike enthusiasm they apply to all public spectacles — which appears charming or touching depending on the quality of the show. They are easily spotted. They applaud like Max Beerbohm's Zuleika, who 'In the way peculiar to persons who are in the habit of appearing before the public, held her hands well above the level of her brow, and clapped them with a vigour demonstrative not less of her presence than of her delight.'

All actors leave during the tea interval. Those performing are obliged to work waiters' hours, the others are terrified people might imagine they are not.

In the years when Surrey CC and the rest of the country never had it so good, I enjoyed the honour of sitting below the immemorial gas-holders and sharing my packet of sandwiches with a star player of C. Aubrey Smith's Hollywood XI.

The glittering Hollywood magnet has many facets. It draws genius, ability, looks, sexiness, craftiness, and ambition and hope, if equally empty. Boris Karloff appeared in Hollywood because it was at the end of the railroad track he was being paid to lay. Then requiring alternative employment, he turned to driving trucks of cement, and acting.

Boris Karloff was William Henry Pratt. He was the brother of Sir John Pratt of the Foreign Office. He readily won selection for the side from C. Aubrey Smith, having been to Uppingham. Tall, square-jawed, romantic-looking, he first made hearts throb rather than flesh creep. He became the Monster of the Universal make-up man — the face which frightened several growing generations is studio copyright. He changed his name. Whoever heard of a Monster called Bill?

'The Monster was such a gentle creature,' Boris reflected over his pint at the Oval. 'If he shuffled about killing people, he simply knew no better.'

He was gentle himself, unloquacious, amusing, thoughtful, knowledgeable about the game, the ideal man to discover sitting in the next seat. The single-minded application of the players to cricket is widened by important personages with a boyish delight in talking to cricketers. Some of these personages are dreadful bores. Luckily, the game provides a higher education in tolerating boredom.

Stewart Surridge's conquering side of the fifties saw refreshing Boris as another former player. Boris was as constrainedly proud of sitting on the team dressing-room balcony as of winning an Oscar. He had a thoughtful wife who met him at the Hobbs Gate on the close of play with a dry martini in a thermos in the glove-locker. He was my fellow-clubman like Ben Travers and Ken More — who used to come

74

on the bus until the conductress kept refusing his fare. Ken asked why. 'Because I love you,' she said.

At the 1964 Oval Test against Australia when Fred Trueman took his 300th Test wicket (Hawke c Cowdrey 14), Boris complained mildly to me that he was falling to bits. The surgeons patched his body together, but sadly not as magically as Frankenstein. He died five years later, aged 81. He achieved one of the 48 foot-square black-and-gold plaques in St Paul's Covent Garden, the actors' church. It is inscribed rightly with Marvell's 'He nothing common did nor mean Upon that memorable scene,' and is positioned at second slip from Ivor Novello.

His memory is as immortal as the ghouls he played. The man from the *Sunday Times*, his mind straying during Sir Michael Redgrave's memorial service, startled himself with the image of Boris with billowing cloak and bared fangs brightening the ritual by rising screaming from under a slab.

C. Aubrey Smith was anticipated by settlers among the Redskins. New York saw cricket before Broad-Halfpenny Down. Cricket and the English language in 1776 were proof against revolution, and the New England XI of 1850 make a handsome bunch on the pavilion walls at Lord's.

The first English touring side, which sailed in 1859, had John Wisden complaining that 'The sea needs ten minutes of the heavy roller'. In August 1872 W. G. Grace — 'the Babe Ruth of cricket' — brought an XI including Lord Harris and A. N. 'Monkey' Hornby aboard the 400-ton *Samaritan* in storms so violently vomitory that W.G. busied himself with his will — necessarily to dispatch in a bottle — while Monkey piled luggage against cabin door to stem the Atlantic, and left-arm Lancashire bowler A. Appleby enthusiastically cheered the white-faced groaning side by singing repeatedly *A Life on the Ocean Wave* and *Home Sweet Home*.

The England XI played the New York, Philadelphia and

Boston XXIIs. They generally won by an innings. Cricket and communism never caught on in America, neither suiting the national character.

Cricket spread like the Australian gum-tree under the bright skies of the British Empire.

Who knew not the Bodyline Controversy for real in the 1930s cannot know how an Englishman wore the idea of Empire as unthinkingly as his clothes. We were everywhere.

'When I was thirteen, we left Germany for China. I remember every stop we made on the *Haruna Maru* — Port Said, Suez, Aden, Bombay, Colombo, Singapore, Hong Kong, and Shanghai. And at every stop the Union Jack was flying and a British officer in knee socks, with a topee and a swagger stick, would come aboard and say, "Howjado",' observed a future Secretary of the US Treasury.

Listening to the Test 50 years ago you knew the BBC was bringing it all the way from Australia. 'Whoooosh whoooom Larwood's running to the wicket eeeepppp wowowowowow Bradman's turned him to leg, good krkrkrkrk, sir!' crackled from the receiver on dim icy mornings to families silent over their porridge. Play stopped when you went to work, a radio being a motoring luxury as *outré* as a cocktail-cabinet, and a portable wireless was the size of a mobile commode.

Those times when flannels were made of flannel, appeals were *sotto voce*, and the Oliver Cromwell was as taboo as the clap, Australians were known only as wearers of green gorblimey caps who said stumps instead of close of play. In 1950 I achieved my childhood dreams. I watched the Test at the Gabba at Brisbane (sticky wicket, England declared 68 for 7 in their first innings, Australia at 32 for 7 in their second and won by 70).

I had arrived embellished with brass buttons, doctor aboard a cargo ship.

In Australia then, afternoon tea meant steak-and-eggs, there was nothing to drink but beer and the police threw

77

everyone out of the pubs at six. Entertainment was 'swy', the gambling game of two-up, which only Australians can appreciate, like their hot meat pies which on biting squirt a gravy like sump-oil. Women had their place in Australian society, codified by defining a wife as 'a gadget you screw on the bed and it does the housework'.

I returned much later as a Literary Gent, to discover Sydney all skyscrapers, opera-house, oysters Rockefeller and Great Western champagne. It has dinner-parties so polite you forget there is nothing between your tulled hostess, who is slicing the pavlova, and Darwin but abos and kangaroos.

Women are now admitted to be part of the natural order less curious than the native duck-bill platypus, the only mammal that lays eggs.

Sydney has discovered vice. While the panting pre-breakfast joggers picked their way through the crumpled tinnies and huddled drunks of Kings Cross, I found ladies of the night facing the morning like bleary vampires. I confessed to an inviting blonde in a black leather bikini it was a trifle early in the day for a Pom. 'But it comes cheaper, sport,' she explained helpfully. How typically practical of Australia, providing sex at matinée prices. I wondered if she gave half fare to OAPs.

Near Hobart hangs a road sign, DEVONSHIRE TEAS. The southernmost tea and crumpets in the world. Which is the charm of Australia. It assures you there'll always be an England, even if it is in Tasmania.

Before the First World War half of Britain's savings were invested abroad, much in the Empire. Before the Second World War British overseas investments paid for a quarter of our imports. Rightly or wrongly, we lived off the world nicely — until we had to sell the lot to America to pay for the war against Hitler. As we were both on the same side, this seems hardly cricket.

Without the Empire we should never have enjoyed the

vaguer values of the Commonwealth, nor this poem in the *Pink 'Un* after the 1896 Old Trafford Test:

> For 'twould have been a sorry game
> Without those runs of Ranji's;
> And Father Thames was glad to claim
> His tributary Ganges.

(Prince Ranjitsinhji made 154 not out)

Tea Interval

The players came off for tea on the overcast, fitfully drizzly second day of a mid-week Middlesex match at Lord's.

A pair of late arrivals took the far end of my empty white bench in the sparsely peopled pavilion, nearest the pitch and behind the bowler's arm. I politely gathered the prudent cricket-watcher's equipment of binoculars, lunchbox, drinks-cooler, thermos-flask, corkscrew, ballpoint, newspaper, scorecard, paperback, mackintosh, umbrella, sun hat, dark glasses, pullover, transistor and Wisden.

The beef-faced, middle-aged one in a tweed suit immediately rose again, announcing, 'I've just remembered, Charles — the members' bar's open all afternoon. Don't know about you, but I'm off for a glass of beer.'

'Do, my dear fellow,' piped his companion. 'I'll just stay and take in the scene.'

He was old, pale, wrinkled, with whispy white hair and a white moustache seeming rusty at the edges. He had thick round glasses and a threadbare blue suit with spotty lapels, thrice buttoned down the front. His tie was frayed, his shoes marbled. I suspected him a retired business acquaintance, or old employee afforded an outing from some seedy old folks' home.

The little old man sat with knobbled hands under sparse

thighs, leaning forwards to stare intently across the white rail, nervously screwing round to glance at the Long Room windows, the balcony, the sightscreen.

I felt he needed comforting.

'Slice of cake, sir?'

'Oh! How very kind. Dundee! Irresistible.'

I unscrewed my flask.

'Tea, if you don't mind a shared cup?'

'The cake will appease me perfectly.'

The slice in both hands, he nibbled as a squirrel a nut.

'Frequently at Lord's, sir?'

'My first visit.' His bright blue eyes twitched round the ground. 'Which I may mitigate by the further confession this has been my lifelong ambition. After all, it's a national monument, like the Albert Memorial. Is the game interesting?'

'Extremely. Six wickets since lunch. The ball's swinging, you see.'

'Swinging? What does that mean, precisely?'

Such earnestness demanded care in reply.

'In these damp, cloudy conditions the ball swings as it comes down the pitch. Sometimes in, sometimes out. The bowler can control this, confusing the batsman, who offers the wrong stroke and gets out. You see?'

'Fascinating.' His pebble-glasses fixed me.

'More fascinating because the weather really has nothing whatever to do with it.'

He was intrigued.

'I did a bit of physics at university,' I mentioned, 'I am a doctor. And I've studied the aerodynamics of the cricket ball. I'll explain ... '

I broke off apologetically, 'Perhaps you'd find it boring, if it's a bit beyond you?'

'I can only applaud such courtesy, I'm sure characteristic of members of your club.'

I set the field of my thoughts.

'The movement of a cricket ball through some twenty yards of air is affected by five factors.' I ticked my fingers. 'The speed. The shape of the ball. The polish on one side of it. The

81

prominence of the seam. And the angle of the seam to the flight path.'

'Really?'

'Let us consider a perfectly smooth sphere moving through an entirely non-viscous fluid — er, gasses are of course to physicists fluids. The pressure on the sphere is lowest where the velocity of the fluid is highest, on its sides. This is Bernoulli's theorem.'

'Bernoulli's,' he muttered, nodding the name into his memory.

'The Bernoullis in the mid-eighteenth century,' I expanded, 'were an amazing Swiss family of scientists and mathematicians. Two generations, Jacques and Jean, Nicolas and Daniel. It was Daniel's theorem which stated that the pressure energy and the kinetic energy of a fluid particle remain constant.'

I added smilingly, 'Forgive me for being technical. It's a fundamental principle of aerodynamics. Isaac Newton had tried working it out from birds, but he got the sums wrong'

I sipped my tea.

'But real air is viscous, sticky. And a real cricket ball develops a "boundary area" of slow-moving air against its rough surface. This exists in two states — the *laminar*, which is steady and parallel to the ball's surface, becoming the *turbulent*, full of random variations.'

I invited, 'When you get home turn on a tap, and you'll notice the smooth flow breaks up earlier the faster the water. The moment of change — that is, from laminar to turbulent flow — depends on something scientists call the "Reynolds number", which I will not muddle you with.'

I threw in, 'Though if you're interested, it was postulated by Orborne Reynolds at Manchester in 1883.'

'You're very well informed,' he congratulated me.

'More cake?'

'Thank you, no.'

'Where was I? This critical Reynolds number, when the smooth flow breaks up, would not be reached by a sphere the size of a cricket ball under 80 miles an hour, which is touched

only by top West Indian bowlers. But there are complications.'
'I'm sure there are.'
'A cricket ball is not smooth and symmetrical. It has a seam.'
'I am at least aware of that.'
'Four lines of stitches with fundamental effect on the ball's behaviour. It happens to be just the size to "trip" the laminar boundary layer I just mentioned into turbulence, so it remains stuck for longer to the ball. There is a shorter wake. There is less drag. I do hope all this is not too complicated for you?'
'Oh, not at all.'
'Let us come to practical cricket. The bowler angles the seam of the ball across the line of its flight, so the seam trips the boundary area *on one side only*. If the speed of the ball is slow enough, for the Reynolds number to be low enough, for the boundary area on the *other* side to remain normal . . . ' I took breath. 'The pressure of the air is reduced on the seam-affected side *only*, and the ball swerves to that side. Get it?'
'I do,' he told me eagerly.
'Good! Thus a ball with the seam angled towards the slips would swing away from the batsman towards them, the "outswinger" as we cricketers call it. And one with the seam facing fine leg would be an "inswinger".'
'I should never have imagined so much science involved in a beautiful game with no purpose but the amusement of its participants and spectators.'
'You've probably grasped by now that swing bowling must be *under* 80 miles an hour — that old Reynolds number again! So fast bowlers are not swing bowlers. The real quickies deviate the ball only by angling the seam to hit the ground in different ways.'
'And how more subtle a game than I imagined! No wonder it is capable of holding entire nations spellbound for days on end.'
'But a fast bowler's ball can of course swing *after* hitting the ground. Because then it is abruptly slower, and all the factors I've been explaining which cause swing come into operation. Follow? Similarly, a swing bowler can propel the ball at a speed

83

which slows to the critical Reynolds number when well on its way — "late swing". Do you know why bowlers have red stains on their trousers?'

'Because they polish one side of the ball only.'

'Congratulations!' I smiled condescendingly. 'This simply emphasizes the mechanism I outlined to you — of a smooth flow on the smooth side and a turbulent flow on the other and rough one. Now, spin.'

'Ah, spin!'

'We come to the Magnus effect.'

'Do we?'

'It was discovered in 1853 by Professor Magnus, of Berlin.'

'Um, Berlin.'

'You've been there?' I inquired politely.

'Never. But like many of my generation, my attention was focused on the place for five or six years during the earlier forties.'

'Quite. We all had to do our bit. For the spin bowler, the seam on the ball is its cog-wheel. He grips the seam to spin it, so it will break in a different direction to its flight when it bites into the ground.'

'Oh, I know that much.' He seemed mildly hurt.

'I'm sure you do. But the slow bowler can in addition move the ball in the air, delivering it with a low-scoring Reynolds number. Consider the ways a cricket ball can spin.'

I twirled my forefinger. 'One, it can spin on an axis *parallel* to its line of flight, like the turbine of a jet-engine. Two, it can spin on an axis at *right angles* to its line of flight, like a bicycle wheel revolving round its hub. Third, it can spin on an axis which is *perpendicular* to its line of flight, as if the batsman had a child's humming-top coming at him through the air.'

'Rather well put,' he complimented me.

'Thank you. Now, it's the humming-top axis which invokes the Magnus effect. The air flow is squashed on the side of the ball towards which it is spinning. Hence the pressure on that

84

side of the ball is lower. Hence the ball will drift towards that side. Savvy?'

'Savvy.'

'You may be interested that this effect which we can observe every day at cricket was utilized by Göttingen University scientists in the 1920s to propel a ship. They chopped the masts off a schooner and erected tall rotating cylinders, and it went bobbing over the Baltic. Pity it never caught on. Would have made quite a change in Cowes Week.'

'You never know what the Germans will get up to next.'

'Indeed. So you see, the spin bowler can either go for the Magnus effect and deceive the batsman with the flight. Or propel the ball like a jet plane and fox the batsman with the break. Or a bit of both. Though I don't think they work it out with graph-paper in the dressing-room. If it doesn't come naturally to a man, he might as well concentrate on his gardening.'

I scowled at the sky. 'Did you feel a spot of rain? I do hope your pilgrimage to Lord's won't be washed out.'

'I've already found it highly entertaining.'

'So glad. Cricketers haven't much patience with fancy theories, of course. When the great W. G. Grace defined his principles of play, he said, "Putting the bat against the ball." Bowlers respond with a pitying grin and say that everyone knows the ball will swing when the skies are grey, or the tide comes in at Scarborough or Hove, or when the smell like hot Marmite wafted across the Oval from the sauce-factory at the Vauxhall end.'

'I'm sure that even the most eminent scientist would be more foolish than arrogant to dismiss the significance of popular beliefs.'

'That's very wise of you,' I said approvingly. 'We doctors constantly find examples. Had William Withering in the eighteenth century not listened to the country bumpkins who cured the dropsy with foxglove tea, we should never have seen the science of cardiology which brings you all those interesting operations of television.'

The old man sat hunched, staring across the pitch with a satisfied smile.

'Nevertheless,' I continued firmly, 'the only possible effect of humidity is swelling the seam, so slightly increasing the turbulence of that boundary layer I mentioned. And making the varnish tacky, encouraging the spin a little.'

The umpires came down the steps beside us.

I packed away my thermos. 'If I am mystified at modern bowlers' enthusiasm for complaining about the ball — which the more asymmetrical the better it swings and the odder it bounces — I'm sure the purely practical W. G. Grace would have been, too.'

I added helpfully, 'There was an article about all this in the *New Scientist* five or six years ago. If you're interested, I'm sure your public library could dig you out a copy. I don't expect you'll find the scientific jargon too much for you. Here's your friend.'

The beef-faced man pushed along the row of seats, followed by a tall pale one in a corduroy jacket.

'Charles, I ran into an old acquaintance from Cambridge who'd like to meet you.'

The newcomer simperingly proffered his scorecard.

'Might I ask you to sign this, Lord Wallingford? It'll be the only scorecard in history autographed by a Nobel Prizewinner who did all the British work on the atom bomb.'

Cricket and Shakespeare

THE LITERATURE OF CRICKET flows as beautifully as the literature of love, but more cheerfully.

I seek it in the London Library. This is a chink in the western corner of St James's Square, narrow storeys of stories among girders, steep steel stairs and latticed metal catwalks, like a bookish Second World War cruiser.

Here gather the English *literati*, who — being English — create so clubby an atmosphere that meeting another man of letters I have murmured absently across the book-issuing counter, 'And a couple of gin-and-tonics, please, miss.'

The London Library of course has a cricket team, which plays in Regent's Park.

'Cricket' is lumped under 'Science and Miscellaneous', a bracketing expressing the traditional disdain of literary persons for those who make stinks and know how machinery works.

I picked out *Phoenix from the Ashes* by Mike Brearley, *The Ashes* by Ray Illingworth and Ken Gregory, *Ashes in the Mouth* by Ronald Mason, *Ashes to Ashes* by H. R. Haweis, *Defending the Ashes* by P. G. H. Fender, and *In Quest of the Ashes* by D. R. Jardine.

I first opened *Ashes to Ashes*.

87

It was a melancholy autumn night. I had strayed on to the beach, and stood watching the foamless but still heaving waters as they lifted up great masses of tangled sea-weed and shells, torn from the rocks during the late storm. The last glimmer of light from the sunset had faded out upon the sea.

It seemed like a disappointing end to the season. I turned the pages.

You may not smell them, but they are there; or you may smell them. Your Marylebone graveyard, closed for more than thirty years, smells; your St John's Wood graveyard smells; your suburban cemeteries smell.

I was outraged. England had fielded some pretty poor teams against Australia at Lord's since the Ashes were instituted in 1882, but such virulent criticism was *not* cricket.

I irritably flicked to the end.

The public sigh for the pure and simple disinfectant of Fire, the reign of Cremation, and the Field of Rest.

I looked at the title-page.

It was published in 1875, and H. R. Haweis was not a lurid Australian quickie but an English clergyman. In the mind of the London librarians, 'Cremation' comes immediately before 'Cricket'. It is salutary to be reminded that in the midst of even sporting life we are in death.

How sad that the Gamesmanship Research Council, Cricket Division, was silenced before its Report could reach the shelves of the London Library by that of Stephen Potter.

The Great Gamesman wrote little on cricket. He left advice for batsmen to acquire ambidexterity, go in eighth wicket, and irritatingly force an already weary field to change position by playing balls alternately right- and left-handed. He advised one bowler to achieve mimicry of the umpires' voices and shout 'No ball!' at the moment of delivery. 'The gambit got him an occasional wicket, but it was frowned upon by the older generation of gamesman.'

'Spectatorship', or 'the art of winning the watching', is similarly but fragmented flotsam on the seas of English Literature. The surviving ploy of enclosing *Wisden* in the cover of *Bradshaw's Railway Guide*, winning arguments by recalling ancient bowling figures to two places of decimals while pretending to look up the train home, has the unfaded Edwardian charm of Sherlock Holmes.

Stephen Potter was austere-faced, donnish-mannered and imposingly tall — all three of them affectations. He sat assessing the game with masterful solemnity, exclaiming sporadically, 'I say! Look how that one swung!' or simply, 'Well bowled!' and winning applauding nods from spectators all round who probably knew as little about cricket as he did.

He was first a guerrilla gamesman in the literary jungle, a critic. I suspect that I am one of his 'Men who have kept a small talent on the boil for so long that there is nothing left but the vapour.' (The temptation to turn the gas on again is irresistible.) His wife initiated life's greatest gamesmanship, running a marriage bureau.

When I sat at the Oval with Stephen Potter and Boris Karloff the trams had already entered eternal peace. In my early cricketing years they ground past the mid-wicket boundary like travelling greenhouses, decorated with advertisements for life's forgotten essentials like Virol and Parish's Food and Sunlight Soap, bells chiming lugubriously to the virtuosity of the driver's foot. If you lacked a Test match ticket you bought a 1s. all-day tram one, following the game through the vast, lurching upper-deck windows over the low Oval wall, hopping on and off a No 40 at the Vauxhall and Pavilion ends in the Harleyford Road. It was the precursor of TV, if more strenuous.

My original publisher was among the last of all original publishers. They shortly conglomerated, as forgotten, charming little railways like the London, Brighton & South Coast are merged into beastly big BR. Michael Joseph's firm did not know exactly what to make of a doctor who wrote books, nor I of them. At their offices in Bloomsbury (the publishers' Harley Street) the loo had been refurbished, and finding myself there I wrote on the convenient sheet of paper that I certified it as sanitary. Michael Joseph immediately framed it and hung it over the apparatus. This was my first inkling of having arrived as an author.

Michael was rightly more fond of his cats than his authors. A lovely summer Sunday afternoon at his country house was thunderstruck by a car hitting his favourite. I was urgently summoned to the case. I applied the usual tests and pronounced it dead.

Michael was far more distressed than had I been the victim, and undeniably I represented greater earning-capacity to him than the cat. I led him from the corpse, arm round shoulders, using the too-practised doctor's technique of comforting the bereaved. The cat got up and walked away. Michael Joseph never again regarded my books with wholehearted confidence.

My next publisher was Alan Lane. He advertised my four Penguins in the Tube, competing with those comely girls in Kestos bras on the escalators who titillated my earliest cricketing days.

Alan Lane was a smiling, nervously hand-rubbing modest man who could never make up his mind. He was not the benevolent mass-educator, the Dr Barnardo of the intellect. He grasped that the public wanted cheap plain books, and the principle of Somerset Maugham's observation, 'If you can give the masses a good thrilling story and let them think at the same time that they are improving their minds you'll make a fortune.'

The storm over *Lady Chatterley's Lover* had filled his sails, the Penguin warehouse was crammed with it, labelled for every town in the Kingdom with a bookshop. He printed *The*

Trial of Lady Chatterley, and sent it instead of Christmas cards.

Twenty-five years later, it reads with the logical lunacy of *Alice*. A trial is ridiculous for obscenity. Like constipation, it is a matter of personal standards. The evil that men do lives in their skulls, and anyone so disposed will go out to commit rape and pillage inflamed by nothing but views of the Lake District. And pornography spreads such pleasure — among those enduring national figures who, as E. F. Benson of Rye noticed, 'Trumpeted their horror, like great moral elephants piously running amok.'

'Life is like a night in an old-fashioned pub,' Alan Lane told me. 'It gets better towards closing time.' He became an earnest slimmer, long before Penguins went into diet books. He booked a room in the London Clinic and ate nothing for days. His response to the announcement of his knighthood deserves imitation. He was so overcome he went to bed for a week.

My work has since appeared under many imprints, the latest St Michael. It is agreeable for an author to be published by his tailor.

'But it is in this consideration which he enjoys that the successful author finds his richest reward. He is, if not of equal rank, yet of equal standing with the highest; and if he be open to the amenities of society, he may choose his own circles. He without money can enter doors which are closed against almost all but him and the wealthy.' Trollope exposes the prime charm of an author's lot with refreshing plainness.

This has brought me valued access to county dressing-rooms, the President's box at Lord's, and the crowded cabin atop the pavilion haunted by the high spirits of Johnners, Old Bloers, The Bearded Wonder, Sir Frederick, Jenkers, The Alderman and The Boil.

Many having the same idea of authors as Trollope, I get letters asking how to be one.

91

Some say: 'My teacher has set me a project on your life, so please send full details and what motivates you to write your books, thanking you in anticipation, Ron Blewitt (aged 13).'

I reply: 'Mr Gordon is abroad for several years, F. Wigglesworth, Secretary,' and feel like Herod on the morning after.

Others ask how to get a grant.

I assert that a man who writes a book needs at least the intelligence to hold a job, and suggest one in a bank like P. G. Wodehouse and T. S. Eliot.

The intending author should look upon the world as his oyster and comprehensive school. The cleverest write for the Third Form, whose educational void makes difficult to display the comparisons and reflections necessitated in telling a story.

The Third are a tough lot. Molière read his comedies to his housekeeper in the chimney corner, foretelling the reception of the play from its reception at the fireside. Whenever the old woman laughed, the audience always would. S. J. Perelman never forgot Groucho Marx's Barber in Peru — not South America but Peru in Midwestern Indiana, its barber 'exhausted from his day's work and attended by a wife and five children, staring vacuously at the screen and japes he could not understand'.

It is easier writing for the Sixth Form, who would never be discovered reading a Third Form book, however technically brilliant, even on the loo.

God knows who I write for. The science O-level resits, perhaps.

The only cricket in Shakespeare chirps.

Close of Play

Two o'clock on Sunday morning.
Terror!
I woke.
Agonizing pain, right behind the sternum.
The dreaded coronary!
I gasped.
Fifty years a cricketer, and this was the close of play.
A blinding light!
How often have patients croaked, 'I see a blinding light,' and gone out like one.
Thunder. Boooom!
A slim blonde in sky-blue voile with well-preened wings said in a British Airways voice: 'Prepare to meet thy God, sir.'
We were alone under a vast glittering gold dome.
'Would you care for a complimentary glass of champagne, sir? We are serving today the Dom Pérignon 1715.'
'How kind.'
I took the glass from her silver tray. The sparkling fluid disappeared.
'But what happened?'
'You drank it, sir. Tomorrow morning's paper, sir?'
'No, thank you. Yes!'

94

I fumbled for the obituaries. Nothing. I recalled despondently the remark of ex-bank clerk Eliot, 'Our life is unwelcome, our death Unmentioned in *The Times*.'

I handed it back. 'May be in the day after's, I suppose.'

'We have every copy of *The Times* until 29 November 2025, sir.'

'What happened then?'

'It was suppressed by the Government, sir. Do you hold a British passport?'

'Of course. But why?'

'God wears many faces, sir, and likes to vary Himself to meet national requirements. If you desire any assistance the celestial staff will be pleased to help you. We shall shortly be serving lunch.'

I confessed awkwardly: 'It's silly, but I always imagined God like a bulky, peppery but obviously very decent senior member of MCC with a gingery beard, who often sat near me outside the Long Room at Lord's.'

She gave an angelic smile. 'We shall see, sir, shan't we?'

Thunder. Boooom!

He was. Same chap.

I was in an enormous stark marble-floored office. God wore a houndstooth suit, Tattersall check shirt and glistening MCC tie. He was on the telephone.

'I know who *everyone* is,' he was explaining gruffly. 'I can do something about your grandmother but the cat'll have to take its chances. Anything else while you're on your knees? *Do* speak up, right ho.'

He inspected me over his half-moons.

'People mumble so at prayer, Me knows why. Take a pew. Cigar? Cigarette? It doesn't matter any more, of course.'

I sat facing His bare marble desk.

'You talk to the whole world with only two phones?' I inquired wonderingly.

'The red one's direct to Hell. The hot line.'

'Haven't I seen you at Lord's?'

'I expect so. I am everywhere.'

He folded His hands on the blotter.

'Afraid someone down the chain of command, on whom the wrath of Me will shortly descend, has made a cock-up of your case. You see, we had a perfectly straightforward classification of the quick and the dead, until you doctors mucked it up. Resuscitation, I mean. There's people knocking about here for months on end while they're breathing away on some beastly ventilator down below, they get very upset, wouldn't you if you'd lost your luggage?'

I exclaimed joyfully, 'I'm still wired up to TV screens, surrounded by busy doctors and nurses?'

'That's right. You're going to be OK, though I must say you've got them pretty worried at the moment.'

I calculated, 'A lot of people must come and go like this.'

'Indeed. It all makes work, you know. We've developed a routine. The public suffering from what you doctors call "recoverable arrests" are issued with a cheap day return. We stick them in the Limbo Room, Florence Nightingale gives 'em a dose of lethe, they're back home and no harm done. But you seem to have ended in eternity, I do apologize. Will you join Me for lunch?'

Thunder. Boooom!

I was in a vast restaurant made of glass. It was revolving slowly amid fleecy clouds in a bright blue sky. There was musak, harp.

'We've none of that time and space stuff up here, you know,' God apologized.

We took a corner table.

He picked up the parchment menu. 'The fricassee of pterodactyl is very good. Morning, Mabel.'

A white-gowned winged waitress materialized.

'My guest had hot lobster last night, so is about to choose a manna omelette,' He instructed her. 'I'll have a mammothburger.'

96

I murmured, 'A glass of the house of God wine would be very nice.'

'Yes, it's very reliable, my son's in the business.'

He broke bread.

'What's your view on the Bishop of Whatsit, who keeps making such an ass of himself?' He invited.

'Wants to be a hit on TV, like other important people.'

God snorted. '*Self*-important, I'd say.' He added gloomily: 'My ministers aren't what they were, that's as plain as an archbishop's crook. Fault of you doctors and scientific chappies.'

I beseeched forgiveness.

'Look, in the old days, where could a bright lad soak up the gravy with his ambition? The law and the church, finish. Wolsey, Luther, name any Pope, clever chaps. Now you cream 'em off to split atoms and such nonsense. Small wonder people don't give much for the word of Me. Ah, we're about to receive our lunch, for which I am truly thankful.'

The waitress set before me a succulent steaming omelette on a gold plate. It disappeared.

'Where's my omelette gone?' I complained.

'You've eaten it.'

I shrugged. 'It must be trying, knowing absolutely everything?'

God waved a hand airily. 'I delegate. I've a tip-top team of apostles and morale is excellent among the saints. I never need fuss over your infinitesimal bit of my creation.'

'You mean our earth?'

'No, I mean your universe.'

God glared. 'Me! There's that frightful Frog Voltaire.'

Through the glass doors came a skinny man with a nutcracker face in a yellow brocade coat and curly silver wig.

The newcomer laughed, flicking a lace-fringed hand. 'The mind of man made God as well as His cathedrals, *n'est-ce pas?*'

97

'I'm fed up with his sneery jokes about inventing Me,' God muttered crossly. 'I said to him, see George Berkeley — *there's* a bishop for you! — and you'll learn pretty smartly that *everything* exists only in My mind. *I am always about in the Quad, And that's why the tree Will continue to be,* remember?'

I nodded politely.

'Voltaire — it's not even his real name — had the cheek to suggest that both George *and* I only existed in *his* clever-dick mind. Philosophers! I've no control over anyone once they're up here, of course,' He added regretfully. 'Personally, I think he's a nutter. I'd have Sigmund take a look at him, except *he* has the cheek to try analysing *Me*. That's the trouble with you doctors — always playing Me.'

A big red-faced man in a golden gown swept past our table, saying jovially: 'I'll join you for an ambrosia after.'

I asked: 'Who's that?'

'Jove.'

I frowned.

God explained: 'We're all in the same business, aren't we? The Olympians are sort of ITV and we're BBC, and like the BBC we know we're holier. Their ratings took a dreadful tumble when I started my big campaign back in 0000, but . . .' He sighed. 'However brilliantly the Rome office organizes My fan club, things have gone off. You doctors have taken away a lot of business. Half the dead of fifty years ago are now the elderly and filling up your buses in the mornings. Buddha's around somewhere, but he usually uses the takeaway.'

I felt God needed consoling. 'But folk go on inviting you to their weddings and christenings and funerals.'

He nodded. 'Yes, they still think the big occasion's not the same without Me, but the competition's terrible. There's so many more places to go than Church. Your Darwin didn't help, muddling Me with a monkey. But what can you expect of a chap who spends the best five years of his youth bobbing

98

round the world in a highly uncomfortable little boat? Though I'm glad people aren't so frightened of Me these days,' He reflected. 'Do you know my undying wish?'

I shook my head.

He leant earnestly across the table.

'That people would credit Me with a sense of humour. They think I'm po-faced. Whoever made a joke talking to Me? But I must have a sense of humour to have created you lot, surely,' He chuckled.

'Some of us end up — ' I pointed downwards.

'Oh, there's always defectors. Some surprising, after a lifetime's cover as respectable and even eminent citizens. We live in peaceful co-existence with Hell, though we're two entirely different ideologies both utterly convinced we're right,' He explained fair-mindedly. 'Just coffee?'

'Thanks.'

'Things got pretty hairy when they shot down one of our angels who strayed into their air-space,' He recalled, as the coffee in my onyx cup vanished. 'We sorted it out somehow. Relations have greatly improved since the War — against the hosts of Satan, you must have seen the report by that poor little blind chap in black, sitting next to Johnson, who's hogging the conversation as usual. Though of course, you never know when some lunatic in Pandemonium is going to press the button, and he's got the most efficient generals in the world down there.'

I asked respectfully: 'Without reaching Miltonic heights, may I write about this? Is it all off the tablets?'

'Authors of your age are always writing about Me,' He replied off-handedly. 'Ingratiation, I suppose. There was an entertaining play called *Outward Bound*; everyone was dead, I dropped into a matinée. Do what you like, dear boy,' He invited genially. 'Convince people I'm still in business. I don't mind an honest atheist, but I can't stand the embittered sort who don't so much disbelieve in Me as personally dislike Me, as said by that lanky chap who wrote *1884.*'

'*1984.*'

'Why quibble? Anything you'd like to see while you're here?'

'Some cricket.'

God smiled broadly. 'One of My happier creations, like spaniels, crumpets and daffodils. We'll trot along to the Elysian Fields, see anyone you like there, Patsy Hendren, Charles Kortright, Jack Hobbs, and we have some very promising players coming up.'

The sky-blue angel was beside me.

'Will you proceed to departure gate 12, sir.'

'Pity,' said God. 'Anything else?'

'Who's going to win the next Aussie Test?'

Thunder. Boooom!

'You've been grunting and groaning so loudly I had to turn the light on,' said my wife crossly, shaking me. 'I *told* you not to choose the hot lobster.'

'I've just been taking lunch with God.'

'Oh, I can quite believe it.'

I informed her smugly, 'So shall I — if we win the next Text match against Australia by six wickets. I intend to bet on it heavily.'

I reflected that God had not imparted if I should be here to see it.

How sad that life has no second innings. I should be perfectly happy to go in last man.